BEST NEW SHORT STORIES

2021

AZ WRITERS

GRANITE PUBLISHING
PRESCOTT & DOVER

ALSO BY AZ WRITERS

Compiled & Edited by Pat Fogarty

Best Poetry— (Nov. 2018)
Best New Poems— (Nov. 2019)
Best New Poems—(2020)

Best Short Stories—Book One (Nov. 2018)
Best Short Stories—Book Two (Dec. 2018)

Best New Short Stories 2019— (Nov. 2019)
Best Short Stories & More— (Feb. 2019)

Best Short Stories—Book One: Large Print Edition (Nov2020)

Best Short Stories—Book Two: Large Print Edition ((Dec. 2020)

* * *

Fogarty, Pat, ed. Best Short Stories 2021 by Az Writers. Prescott.
Cover Photo© Carmina Robles
Granite Publishing, November 2020. Paperback

ISBN: 978-1-950105-16-8
Granite Publishing
Prescott & Dover
9 8 7 6 5 4 3 2 1
First Edition
Printed in the United States of America
HBBXNY 1551065906

FOREWORD

Best Short Stories 2021 by AZ Writers contains 28 captivating stories written by a group of talented authors. The diversity of our authors' backgrounds and their finely honed talent of writing from the heart make this book an excellent choice for anyone who enjoys reading. In this collection, the reader will experience the writing voice and style of many authors. Readers will also find a contemporary multi-genre collection of stories by authors who have a story to tell and the talent to write it. This anthology includes memoir stories, fiction, historical fiction, creative non-fiction, suspense, and many other genres that will amuse, intrigue, and mystify the reader. A few of these stories may make you laugh, and a few may bring a tear to your eye. In this collection, you will find well-crafted stories with irony, adventure, mystery, crime, and a couple of stories with a bit of romance. A superb choice for a cruise, a day at the beach or pool, a long flight, or just to sit at home and have a relaxing read in your favorite chair.

ACKNOWLEDGMENTS

Without the collective efforts of a fine group of writers, *Best Short Stories* 2021 by AZ Writers would never have become a reality. I would like to thank each author who contributed to this project, a truly marvelous group of talented writers.
I would also like to thank photographer Carmina Robles for allowing us to use her copyrighted photo of Granite Mountain for our cover. Pat Fogarty: Editor.

TABLE OF CONTENTS

The Big Boss

Greg Picard

His boss worked three-hundred miles away and nine floors above the earth. Chris Becker thought the lack of oxygen at that elevation affected his brain. The distance prevented his boss from evaluating any issues related to the park district operations anyone was responsible for. The aerial positioning challenged his mood and reasoning.

Besides, he was an asshole. Always was and always would be. At least he was to anyone who worked for him. To those who were his equals or superiors, he was their good buddy. E Clampus Vitus loved his presence as a member. He could outdrink all of them and had more new off-color jokes than the best of them. He was a back slapper and a climber in the organization. He always had a smile and flattery to those he was sucking up to. Chris Becker had watched his meteoric rise in the parks department with amazement until he had to work for him.

No doubt, the man was intelligent enough, but he lacked wisdom and tact. He was good at sucking up to supervisors and the public, but not at taking care of those who worked for him. They were beneath him and were mere peons to order around. In a public group, he'd hide it. In private, he'd cut your legs out from under you without a thought. Chris had seen both sides of him and wasn't looking forward to the phone conversation he needed to have with him now.

"He's on line two," Jane said to him as Chris sat in his office.

"Hello, Jim, thanks for getting back to me. I got your message that you want two of our rangers to help cover the big party you've got going all next week at Sutter's Fort. You know, that's gonna be a real hardship for us here. I've lost one ranger, and we're in our busiest season. It leaves me only one peace officer for ten State Parks along 60 miles of coastline. I was hoping you could find someone else to use to help cover things up your way."

"The director wants those extra rangers here. When a superior says he needs one of your rangers, your job is not to try to talk him out of it. Your job is to say yes, sir! Have them report here tomorrow."

Chris thought they were supposed to be on the same team. He knew several districts that were better staffed and had less visitation and crime to deal with. "Well, I thought I'd ask and see if there was another option."

"Your job is not to ask. Just do." The line went dead. *So much for trusting and using the expertise of your employees and their knowledge of their specific issues,* Chris thought as he slammed the receiver down. So, now he and another ranger would do unpaid double shifts for a whole week because of this guy, and it still wouldn't cover the District adequately.

* * *

Six months later...

"He's coming to demonstrate this himself?" Chris asked his Chief Ranger, Tom Seaton.

"Yeah. You know how hot he thinks he is and how much he loves to play with guns."

"He doesn't come out of the rare air hob-nobbing on the 9th floor. I would've thought he'd have handed it off to a subordinate Rangemaster to handle."

"He's the only expert in his mind, and it gives him a chance to show off and to play cops and robbers," Tom said. "You know him as well as I do. It's all ego."

Chris shook his head. "Okay, guess we'll all see him at the range next Friday then."

* * *

Range days were always relaxed. Staff from his district came together, and they even had adjacent park districts and other agencies join with them in their monthly firearms qualifications. With Jim Tweed there, the mood was more subdued, though as usual, Jim worked hard to glad-hand everyone and joke around.

"We're gonna have some fun here today!"

Chris felt like it sounded more like an order from Jim than an expression of joy.

"Simunition is a great way to get a feel for your comfort level in a shootout with a perp. The bullets are a wax compound filled with a red soap that clearly marks a hit. They say it stings, so you'll wear gloves, and if you want, you can wear your rubber rain gear to make it hurt less if you are a real pussy. You're all in old clothes, and the soap washes out just fine." He scanned the group. "Okay, any questions?"

Blank faces were all around, and everyone started putting on gloves and rain gear.

"Okay, I'll volunteer to be the bad guy," Jim said. "We're gonna do a drunk driver car stop scenario, and 'the guy' (me) will come out with a gun, and you get to do your commands and use cover and make the shoot or don't shoot decisions." He loaded his gun with the Simunition rounds and walked over to his state vehicle...a brand-new Ford Interceptor completely equipped with a light bar and the latest in radio communication. Few of the districts even had those. Some were still driving old decade-old Dodge pickups for enforcement vehicles. The 9th-floor execs needed to patrol for wrongdoers.

"Hey, we've got an extra protective cup here, Jim. Do you want it?"

"Naw, I don't think I need that."

Chris had read up a bit on the simulation rounds and had advised his staff to wear a cup to protect the family jewels just in case.

"So, who's gonna go first in the scenario?"

Chris raised his hand. "I'll go."

"Okay, then! Let's do this," Jim said as he smiled and jogged to the sedan and got in. "Make sure to use your vehicle for appropriate cover now, 'cause I'll be returning fire."

"Oh, I will," Chris said, "you can count on it." The others around him laughed.

Chris positioned himself behind the open door of the patrol truck and using the loudspeaker in it, commanded the driver to step out of the vehicle as he would in a high profile stop where he expected potential violence. Jim got out rather unsteadily and slurred some insults as he pulled the pistol out to fire at Chris.

The next four seconds were priceless. Chris was a very good shot and had been a firearms instructor for the department for many years. He placed six rounds dead center on his target's crotch, and Jim doubled over in pain, falling to his knees and eventually flat out in the mud.

"Go see if the arrogant bastard's still breathing," he said with a smile to Tom.

The Abduction

Neil A. Sram

"What happened to dad?" asked Kane.

"What do you mean?" said his mother standing in the living room watering her ficus and rubber tree plants.

"Look," said Kane pointing to the boots at the end of the driveway.

"Oh my god," said Mrs. Arnold as she opened the screen door and ran down the sidewalk to the street with Kane trailing behind.

She stopped at the curb and looked down at her husband's boots then looked up and down the street.

Kane followed his mother's actions. Not seeing his father, but seeing his boots Kane said, "Where's dad."

"I don't know," said Sheila grabbing her cell phone from a pocket.

"Did dad take the car?" asked Kane.

She shook her head. "No, he went to get the mail from the mailbox."

She dialed her husband's cell phone number and while waiting for him to answer pulled down the mailbox door revealing several letters and flyers. She took them out, looked at each then returned them to the mailbox.

His phone went to voice mail. "This is Bill Arnold. I'm busy or away from my phone. Leave a message and phone number and I'll get back to you as soon as I can."

When the message ended Sheila said, "Bill, this is Sheila, your wife. It's 3:15. Where are you? Call me back, I'm worried."

Kane listened to his mother then said, "Is daddy on the phone?"

Sheila looked down at her son, let out a breath, and said, "No, daddy's not on the phone. I don't have the foggiest idea where he is."

Every fifteen minutes during the afternoon, Sheila called and left a voice message on her husband's cell phone. Each time she sounded more desperate.

She also called his co-workers. None had seen him since leaving work on Friday.

Sheila left Bill's boots at the curb believing he would walk through the door wearing them and give her a plausible explanation as to where he'd been.

When Bill Arnold didn't call and didn't show up for dinner Sheila called his brother. "Ted, have you seen Bill?"

After Ted answered, "No," Sheila thanked him and asked if he'd have Bill call home if he should hear or see him.

After hanging up the phone Kane looked up at his mother. "Is dad at Uncle Ted's?"

She shook her head, "No."

When it turned to dusk, she turned on the driveway and exterior house lights.

It was ten o'clock when she was finally able to get Kane to bed.

She was in her bathroom brushing her teeth when she heard pounding on the front door. Still holding her toothbrush, she rushed to the front door and peered through the security peephole. Even with the porch light on, she could not make out the individual. Not wanting to open the door to a stranger, she shouted through the metal door. "Who is it?"

"It's me," said a voice that sounded like her husband's.

She was still skeptical, so she asked again, "Who is it?"

"Sheila, open the door. It's me, Bill."

"Stand in front of the door," she said unlocking the deadbolt then dialed 911 on her cell phone, but hesitated to push the symbol on her phone to initiate the call.

The individual on the porch moved closer to the door and looked directly at the peephole viewer. "I was abducted. Let me in."

She kept a finger hovering over the telephone symbol on her phone as she slowly opened the metal front door. Looking through the screen door, she asked, "Where's your cell phone?"

"They took it."

The person on the porch looked like her husband, but she still wasn't sure it was him. He was wearing the same clothes as her husband had been wearing earlier in the day, but they were torn, his hair and beard were half-shaved, his arms were bloody with what appeared to be bruises, abrasions, and puncture wounds and he was sockless and shoeless.

Before she would unlock the screen door she asked again, "Who are you?"

The outside light cast an eerie shadow across the face of the individual standing on the porch making identification difficult. "This has been the worst day of my life. Let me in," said the individual.

"What's your Social Security number?"

After twice repeating his nine-digit number, Sheila Arnold unlocked the screen door and stepped back to let her husband enter.

Bill Arnold looked hurriedly back towards the street then quickly entered his house, shut and locked the door.

Sheila could now see that his eyes were bloodshot, his nose was bloody, he had scum on his face, his breath smelled like vomit and his clothes were dirty and nearly shredded like he had crawled on his stomach over barbwire. His hair and beard had been half-shaved, although it looked like some of it had been torn out.

Bill Arnold hobbled into the kitchen, grabbed a tall glass from the cupboard, put it under the faucet, turned on the cold water, and filled it. When it was full, he lifted it to his mouth and drank like someone lost in a desert for a week without water. He refilled his glass and drank it, spilling a little down the front of his torn shirt. He filled the glass a third time, carried it to the kitchen table, and sat down. His eyes darted frantically around as if expecting someone or something to happen that would not be pleasurable.

Sheila stood with her back against the stove and watched her husband. She'd never seen him like this. He looked like he'd been beaten and robbed.

"I called you a dozen times. I was worried. I called our neighbors and your co-workers," said Sheila.

"They took my phone," said Bill.

"Why?"

"How should I know?"

"Who are they?"

"There were dozens of them," said her husband.

She was feeling frustrated by his lack of candor. "Who is them?"

"If I told you, you wouldn't believe me," he said.

"Try me. Your son is very upset."

She moved sideways in the direction of the living room.

"I'm sorry. I need to clean up."

Feeling he was not forthcoming, she said sarcastically, "Do you remember where the bathroom is?"

Bill stared at his wife. "I know where the bathroom is. I haven't been drinking. I was abducted."

"By little green men?" said Sheila her face showing indignation.

"Not men. We need to leave. We need to pack our bags and leave."

"God help us," said Sheila. "You're 6 foot 4 inches, 250 pounds, a former college athlete and you're afraid."

"Aliens, Sheila. I was abducted by aliens, the kind that comes from another planet. Do you understand what I'm saying?"

With her hands on her hips, she said, "Where did they take you - Joe's Bar & Grill, Bubba's Topless, Benjy's Joint?"

"This isn't funny Sheila. I barely got out alive. We need to leave."

"Got out of what?"

"They're going to come after me," said Bill.

"Bill, what did you get out of and what have you gotten us into?"

"One was holding me down while two others touched me, pushed me, probed me, cut me, grabbed my hair and beard, and yanked it out."

"So how did you get away?" Sheila asked.

Bill didn't bother to answer his wife. He stood and tottered to the bathroom leaving the door open so Sheila followed him in.

He turned on the shower, took off his clothes, dropped them on the floor, and stepped into the shower.

With his clothes off, Sheila could see the bruises and abrasions on his feet, legs, arms, neck, and back. His face and head were raw where the hair and beard had been removed. He also had a scar across his chest as if he recently had surgery.

Bill let the water cascade off his head and down his body before taking a washcloth and carefully rubbing his body.

Sheila watched him gingerly scrub his body and noticed every time the washcloth passed over a wound, he would cringe with pain.

She caught him looking out the horizontal window above the shower. "What are you looking at?"

"Looking for them," he said.

"You think they're following you?"

"I'm sure of it. That's why we have to leave."

"Why did they pick you?" asked Sheila.

"I don't' know, but I wasn't the only one."

"So you weren't alone."

"There was a woman," he said as he turned off the shower and looked at his wife. "Do you think I did this to myself?" pointing to his injuries.

"I see. You and a woman were taken captive by little green men."

"I didn't say they were men. They were aliens."

Sheila handed her husband a towel which he used to gently dry off.

She had known Bill since high school, had married him seven years ago, had a three-year-old son, and had seen him tie one on, but this time was very different.

He hung the towel on the rack and staggered to his dresser, put on underwear and socks, and then crossed the room to their closet. He settled on a pair of pants and a short-sleeve shirt, put them on then stepped into a pair of mid-calf hiking boots.

Sheila silently watched him dress. When he left the bedroom she asked, "Where are you going?"

"I have to destroy their portal."

"Their what?" Sheila asked.

"I can't let them come again. Next time they may take all of us. I can't let that happen."

"Where is the portal?"

"In the ravine, across the street," said Bill.

"You mean the vacant lot?"

"Yes."

"I've never seen anything there," said Sheila.

"I hadn't either. They must have just arrived," said Bill.

"What are you going to do?"

"Destroy it," said Bill.

"It's not on our property."

"If I don't ..." Bill's voice trailed off. "We need to pack our bags."

"What makes you think that destroying it will stop whoever or whatever it is that attacked you. Bill, we need to call the police."

"I can't wait for them to come and investigate. We could all be dead by then."

"Bill, you're scaring me," said Sheila. "Let's go to the ER and have you checked out. I don't like those wounds."

Bill looked at his exposed arms; the burns, abrasions, the punctures. He'd already made up his mind on the sequence of events: kill the aliens and destroy their portal, go to the ER then leave town.

He didn't wait for Sheila to respond. He stiffly walked through the house to the garage where he picked up a gallon metal can of Coleman fuel. He returned to the kitchen, found a box of safety matches, and started for the front door.

Sheila looked at her husband carrying the can of gas and thought he was having a nervous breakdown or was on drugs.

She followed him to the front door and then watched him cross the gravel street and disappear into the ravine beyond.

Five minutes later she saw flames rising above the trees and thicket. Fearful that her husband's fantasy to kill the aliens might jeopardize their house, she called 911 and told them that there was a fire on the vacant property across the street from their house.

A few minutes after hearing the first siren, Sheila saw her husband cross the street then enter the house and go directly into the garage with the fuel can.

The sounds of fire engine sirens awakened their son who emerged from his bedroom holding his teddy bear.

The three of them watched from behind their screen door as three fire engines and a dozen men doused the fire Bill Arnold had set. When the firemen began rolling up hoses, Bill shut and locked the front door.

Kane was no longer sleepy-eyed. He looked at his father for the first time since waking up. "Dad, why did you take off your boots? Where were you this afternoon?"

Bill looked at Sheila before answering his son. "I took a little trip, but I'm back."

Just then they heard what sounded like a knock on the front door.

Sheila said, "It's probably the police."

Bill looked at her questioningly.

"I called 911 as soon as I saw the flames. I didn't want it to get out of control, jump the street, and burn our house down."

Bill opened the door expecting to see a policeman, fireman, or both. But instead, he found himself staring at three aliens, standing upright on their lower legs. These aliens looked exactly like the three that had tormented and tortured him earlier in the day.

Bill quickly slammed and locked the front door then scooped up his son and retreated with his wife to the living room.

The knocking continued at the front door, then began at the back door.

Suddenly there was another sound, like glass being cut. They turned slowly in the direction of the new sound and saw the triangular head of a large green praying mantis in each of their living room windows. The creatures'large eyes stared at them, their antennae moving rhythmically as their front legs moved back and forth across the glass like a diamond-edged glass cutter.

A Routine Errand

Cordell Compton

Wednesday, April 12, 1865

"Why don't you pull up a chair, Hill? You sound like an elephant thumping around. You're liable to crash through the floor. My pencils and pens keep falling off the desk with you jarring the whole room. I nearly knocked over my inkwell, trying to grab them."

The speaker took off his wire-rimmed glasses, breathed on the lens, and wiped them off with his handkerchief. He leaned back in his chair, closed tired eyes, and rubbed them gently. The seated gentleman then opened dark eyes that followed his oversized friend blundering around the office.

"I'm sorry, Mr. President." The large man thudded down in a chair beside the president's desk. The chair snarled and groaned in raucous contempt when the man shifted his nearly three hundred pounds in a futile effort to get comfortable.

"I apologize, Sir, for getting upset. I got so steamed when I think what that Michigan congressman said about me – on the floor of the United States House of Representatives no less!"

"Ward, if you haven't learned by now, you need to understand how to let tripe like that run off your back. You're going to blow a gasket if you don't. And if you *do* blow a gasket, you won't be any use to yourself or me."

Ward Hill Lamon tilted his head and watched a beetle crawling toward Mr. Lincoln's desk in the second-floor office at the White House. When the small, unsuspecting insect wandered within distance, Lamon lifted his large boot and crushed the defenseless animal. Another pencil rolled off the president's desk.

Mr. Lincoln resumed an upright position behind his desk after leaning over to watch the execution. "I suppose you wish that were Congressman Baldwin under your boot?"

"Why yes, I do and besides. . . ." The executioner stopped in mid-sentence when he glanced up from wiping the insect's remains from his boot. He looked at Mr. Lincoln's faint smile, deepening creases around his eyes, and halted his outburst. Lamon watched his exhausted, long-time friend for a few moments, then laughed. "You always could get me settled down."

"When you deal with all the shenanigans like I have the past four years, you develop a knack for working with people – especially those you'd rather not."

"I'll do better."

"That's all right, Lamon. We go back a long way. I appreciate all the help you've given me."

Ward Lamon and the Sixteenth President traced their friendship to the early 1850s. Born in Virginia, Lamon went to Illinois at about age nineteen to stay with relatives. Along the way, he "read law" as was the custom, and obtained a law degree from the University of Louisville in Louisville, Kentucky in 1851, one of only three or four law schools west of the Appalachian Mountains. Lamon was admitted to the Illinois Bar soon after getting his law degree. As a member of the Bar and in the course of ordinary events, he met a tall, lanky lawyer living in Springfield, Illinois named Abraham Lincoln, who had moved there from his native Kentucky. Lamon and Lincoln became friends.

Soon after Mr. Lincoln's inauguration as president in March 1861, he appointed Lamon as United States Marshall for the District Of Columbia. Being an assertive person, Lamon took an expansive view of his appointment. Even before that event, he made it his duty to "watch over" Mr. Lincoln as he phrased it.

During the delicate planning of safely transporting the president-elect to the District of Columbia for the inauguration, Ward Lamon tangled with Allan Pinkerton, founder of the Pinkerton Detective Agency. Pinkerton believed he had uncovered an assassination plot to kill Mr. Lincoln when his train passed through Baltimore, Maryland, on its way to D.C. Southern sympathizers heightened tensions in Baltimore touting secession from the United States. Lamon, however, discounted such a plot earning the contempt of Pinkerton, who supposedly called him a "brainless, egotistical fool." Conspiracy or not, Mr. Lincoln passed safely through Baltimore without incident.

"What did you want to see me about, Mr. President?"

"I want you to go down to Richmond and see what options are available about getting the southern states back in the Union. As you remember, the conference that Seward and I had in February at Hampton Roads was unsuccessful. Oh, everyone was kind and cordial with smiles and handshakes all around. But nothing came of that meeting. Alexander Stevens, John Campbell, and Robert Hunter proposed terms I could not accept."

"Pardon me, Mr. President, but if you and Secretary Seward couldn't get those fellows to agree to your terms, what chance do I have?"

"For one thing, the war is over now. As vice president of the Confederate States, Stevens could see the end of the conflict, I believe. But he held out hope that circumstances would change. Campbell and Hunter, being lawyers, were smart enough to know what the future held but did not want to go against the 'party line,' so to speak. Hunter had opposed ol' Jeff Davis on many issues but not enough to break with him."

"So, you think the situation is more favorable now?"

"Yes, I do. For example, I got this report from the War Department yesterday concerning their estimate of the status of the southern states that succeeded. About fourteen percent of the South's population are in major cities that have suffered colossal destruction such as Atlanta, Charleston, Columbia, and Richmond. The farms are devastated, and the war destroyed an estimated forty percent of the livestock and farm equipment. Their transportation system, such as it was, is shot to pieces. The banking system and currency are worthless. The barter system is about all that's keeping things going. And with the slaves freed, the plantation owners' wealth evaporated; they have scarce resources with which to start over. They will probably have to revert to parceling up their plantations to sharecroppers.

"The Union won the war, but at what cost to the country as a whole? There is so much repair work to be done on many levels. We have to reach out to those folks and help them back on their feet so they can start over."

"And you think I can help with that effort?"

"You can't do all by yourself, Lamon, but I want you to present the initiative so these fellows can start talking and thinking about their future. We owe them that much at least."

"We do have much for which to be grateful, Mr. President. Do you have any instructions about how you would like me to handle this matter?"

"No, I do not. I'll leave that to your discretion. You will probably get a better understanding of the situation when you get there and talk with them. Some of those gentlemen, however, have tempers and sometimes go off halfcocked – like a few of my other friends." Mr. Lincoln smiled as he peered over his glasses at Lamon.

"All right, Sir, I'll go there with an open mind and listen to what they have to say. Would you like me to wire you my impressions and any possible solution?"

"No, I trust your judgment.

"Do they know I'm coming?" asked Lamon.

"Not yet. I'll have Hay or Nicolay send them a wire."

"Fine. When do I start?"

Mr. Lincoln scratched his chin and shuffled some documents on his desk as he often did while in thought. He looked up and said, "Let's see, this is Wednesday, April 12. Can you get started after lunch?"

"Yes, I can."

"It's a little over a hundred miles or so to Richmond. The roads are muddy from what I've heard with all the rain we've had lately. You probably will have to stop somewhere for the night. If all goes well, you should be able to get there on Friday at the latest."

"That should not be a problem, Sir," said Lamon as he stood beside the president's desk and shook hands. Both men were nearly the same height, but Lamon's girth was more substantial.

"I almost forgot to ask, Mr. President, do you and Mrs. Lincoln have any plans to relax this weekend now that the war is over?"

"No, Ward. Mary's not been feeling well lately, and too much activity bothers her. I asked her about a carriage ride, and she said,'No.' But I might take in a play if I can get caught up with the paperwork."

"Sir, I would encourage you to take some time for yourself. The paperwork, appointments, and visitors will always be there. They can wait."

"You're probably right. I might go to the theater later this week."

Ward Hill Lamon put his hand on the doorknob to leave the president's office. But he pivoted and faced the president who sat at his desk. "Mr. President, on second thought, I'd encourage you to stay close to the White House for a spell. There are too many Southern sympathizers and crackpots still running around the city. Stay home."

Mr. Lincoln was reading letters, making notes on some of them. He paused from his work and looked at Lamon. "Thanks, Ward, I'll keep that in mind."

Lamon hesitated momentarily, looked back at the president, and exited the office. It was a few blocks from the White House to Lamon's boarding house on H Street between 11th and 12th Streets, Northwest. Dodging muddy puddles and horse droppings while he walked, Lamon thought of his friendship with Mr. Lincoln. He remembered their first acquaintance and other events over time. By the time Lamon opened the fence gate of the boarding house, he was thinking of the nights he had slept outside the president's bedroom door at the White House. *That floor was hard. But no one was going to get past me and hurt my friend.*

Ward Lamon was well-known around town for his official capacity as well as for his close friendship with the president. He was not above using either as leverage when it was to his advantage. The newly built buggy he rented was a result of casually mentioning to the stable owner he was on a "personal mission" for the president. His imposing physical presence frequently intimidated people without uttering a word.

For a change, the day was sunny and warm. But Lamon wore his "travel coat" as he called it because of the mud splatters from the horses' hooves. Struggling to keep the horses working together plus battling the mud and heat, Lamon tired much sooner than usual.

It was almost dusk, and he found a small inn near Garrisonville. The stable hand parked the buggy inside the barn behind the inn; the lad brushed and fed the horses. Lamon paid the innkeeper and settled down in the dining room for the evening meal. The steak dinner and baked potato revived him. After some brandy and cigars together with lively conversation with other guests by the fireplace, Lamon was relaxed and ready for bed.

Thursday, April 13, 1865

Lamon slept soundly and awakened before dawn. A hurried breakfast tasted delicious: a slab of bacon, fried eggs, grits, and a pot of coffee energized Lamon for the day ahead. The road south toward Richmond had dried overnight as a bonus. Near lunchtime, Lamon parked the buggy by the roadside and wolfed down a sandwich the innkeeper's wife made for him. By nightfall, he was near Richmond. Lamon found a small hotel on the outskirts of the city for the night's lodging.

Friday, April 14, 1865

It was mid-morning when Lamon gained admittance to a local judge's stately two-story home after showing his credentials to a pair of Union soldiers guarding the house. A servant ushered Lamon into the first-floor study. Within a few moments, other members of the group arrived. The judge came downstairs to welcome the guests.

Lamon addressed the group. "Gentlemen, as you know, I'm here representing President Lincoln. He is eager to find ways so that our nation can come together again. Toward that effort, he met with several of you who are in this room back in February at Hampton Roads." Lamon lifted his glass in the direction of Stevens, Campbell, and Hunter. "Those efforts were unsuccessful. It behooves all of us to put aside whatever differences we had and work together."

Ward Hill Lamon then seated himself facing the group in a sturdy, comfortable, wingback chair that accommodated his girth without protest or complaint. Other members of the group sipped brandy and puffed cigars as they absorbed Lamon's remarks.

Clearing his throat with a cough, former Confederate vice-president Stevens finally responded. "I appreciate your remarks, Mr. Lamon. After our meeting with Mr. Lincoln in February, I came to believe that he is a kind, sincere man with the good of the country in mind. While some of us may not be able to change our 'spots,' maybe we can at least change our minds."

The discussion continued for the rest of the day, with some of the same thoughts that Mr. Lincoln had outlined to Lamon before he left Washington. There was nothing of substance decided except everyone had a fair idea of the issues facing the group. The judge hosting the meeting invited the attendees to stay for dinner. All declined for various reasons, including Lamon. He indicated the need to return to Washington as soon as practical.

This Friday night in Richmond was quiet. About 9:30 pm, Lamon went to bed and fell asleep almost immediately.

Soon after 11:00 pm, Lamon was startled by loud banging on his hotel door.

"Mr. Lamon, Mr. Lamon, wake up."

Stumbling to the door, Lamon jerked it open. "What do you want? Why'd you wake me up in the middle of the night?"

The massive figure of Lamon that filled the doorframe frightened the night clerk. The faint light from the candlestick illuminated the angry guest.

"I'm sorrow to disturb you, Sir, but a Union officer delivered a telegram from the War Department addressed to you. Here it is." The clerk handed the telegram and candlestick to Lamon and scurried down the hallway.

Lamon slammed the door and thudded down on a chair. He placed the candlestick on the table and tore open the telegram.

Mr. Ward Lamon, Richmond, Virginia
URGENT

Mr. Lincoln shot tonight at Ford's Theater STOP He lingers near death STOP Secretary Seward also gravely wounded STOP Possible Conspiracy Afoot STOP Return to Washington AT ONCE, repeat AT ONCE STOP

Edwin M. Stanton

Edwin M. Stanton
Secretary Of War

Redemption

Susan Lanning

The July sun hadn't topped the horizon of the Chiricahua Mountains as Ora Hatcher rose to dress for chores. The long stretch of cloud in the blue sky filling his window was a burning red. Every day took more out of him to get up since his wife's death four years ago. Bea was what he'd made the effort for. She'd given the labor meaning all these years. Hard, without her. By God, it was hard.

As he grabbed overalls off the ancient rocker he heard the hushed voices and the feet beating a retreat through the barnyard and off toward the north. He lunged at the window in time to see the backs of a dozen or more race off through the orchard to the open ground beyond.

"Sons-a-bitches," he yelled after them. "No good, thieving wetbacks!"

Ora pulled on his overalls and stumbled through the house. He stepped into the boots by the front door and grabbed his rifle. Tearing open the door, he ran down the steps toward the back of the house. His eyes, blurry with over sixty summers of Arizona sun, searched the orchard and the field beyond. The ancient hound sauntered out the open door and stood beside him.

In the distance, he made out the figures moving toward a line of brush to the north. "Goddamn greasers," he yelled. Throwing his gun to his shoulder, he let off two rounds in their direction. The early morning air rang with the sound and a flock of finches fluttered and squawked from the cottonwood beside the house. The blue sky, streaked with fire, hung silent as the ringing dissipated.

Ora lowered his gun and remained where he was a moment, seething, staring at where the Mexicans had gone. Spitting off in the dirt, he marched toward the barn and the small kitchen garden beyond. The dog followed.

The barn door gaped wide. Beside it, the wire fence to the chicken pen was trampled and several hens had escaped into the yard.

"Shittin', no good wetbacks. Steal ya blind."

He did his best to prop up the fence before more chickens escaped. After that, he went into the barn. Hay cluttered the floor, the gate for his cows hung busted on one hinge, the heifer and his two milk cows roamed loose, eating the meal on the floor that spilled from gaping slashes in the sacks, the udders on one of the cows still wet where she'd been milked. The mare was in her stall but restless.

"Goddamn it," he barked and shooed the cows back into their stalls, propping the gate closed as best he could. "Good for nothing scavengers," he cried at the hayloft. Rage grew, filling his head until his eardrums bulged with it.

He strode out to the small kitchen garden he still kept for Bea. By now the sun had reached above the mountains, lighting the destruction like a lamp turned on bright. Beans trampled, the plants yanked from the ground, corn stalks broken and stripped bare, squash smashed or half-eaten. Teeth clenched, Ora stared at his back-breaking work destroyed in so brief a time. "Bea, I'm glad you ain't here to see this. It'd break your heart."

Pulling life from the dry earth was like ripping a child from the womb. The heat and the winds fought you, then summer torrents washed half of it away and armies of grasshoppers marched on you to eat everything in sight. And the bank–wanting to foreclose every time your payment was a little late. You had to work until muscle and bone could barely hold you up. And when that didn't do you in, these scavengers, these thieves, these renegades could come in the night and ruin what little was left.

Ora's eyes grew red and hot. He never cried - only once when Bea died. Even at that, his body seemed too dry from the years of sun to form real tears. He shouldered his rifle and headed back toward the house. The dog followed.

Reaching the porch, he heard rustling from a clump of scrub oak to the south. He brought his gun up, pointing in the direction of the sound. No movement. Then, like a flash of light, a figure sprinted across an open space, heading west. Ora's rage blotted out thought. He aimed, steadied his breath, and fired.

The shot split the morning air; the figure in the distance froze until, with the grace of a dancer, it crumpled to the ground.

Ora watched, not moving, trying to understand what he'd just done. Slowly he lowered his gun to his side and took in air. Did he kill the Chicano? Christ, he'd killed people before. Back in Nam, you shot, you killed, you blasted the whole area with bullets just to keep alive. Those sneaking, crawling creatures were like ghouls - invisible until all of a sudden you had a knife in your belly.

Bea had helped him past those years at war, past the nightmares, the sweats, the jumping at noises. Ora thought he'd blow his brains out if Bea hadn't been there, eased him when it got bad, held him at night when the dreams came like bloody ghosts to haunt him. She was patient with his rages and when he sank to his knees in despair, she pulled him to his feet. That was Bea's doing.

But now it was the same thing all over again—the sneaking, the thieving, the crawling through a man's land till it wasn't hardly his anymore. He'd never seen those faces back in Nam. He'd never had to think of them as human. Didn't want to see this face either. Hate burned bright if you didn't look at them. Rage continued to sizzle when you didn't see the results. But it was a mixture - hate for the vermin and hate for yourself for killing, then hate again for them making you kill, and hate for a world filled with killing, even hate for a creator who put them all here.

At last, he walked toward the figure in the distance. The hound already stood by the body sniffing as Ora approached. The Mexican lay sideways, looking to the south toward home for the last time. Blood soaked the ground. Then he saw - not a man but a woman and with a huge bulge in her belly.

"Christ!" he hissed. "Gonna have a baby!"

He all but fell to the ground, his rifle dropping away. Knees up, he buried his face in his hands. "A baby, goddamn it, she's gonna have a child." He lifted his head. "I killed 'em both." The hound gave a long, mournful bay, sounding for all the world like a lost soul in Perdition.

But the lessons of Viet Nam seized him and the hate returned. A baby, she was sneaking across the border to get her child born in the

U.S. so it could be a citizen and suckle at his country's tit. That's what these women did, "You bitching thief, trying to make us take care of your stinking spawn. Ya got no business here. Stay in your own place. Quit trying to steal from me. All-a-ya. Coming over here to take what don't belong to you."

And Bea not able to have kids of her own, not after the miscarriage. Doc said so. It about killed her - her wanting a child so bad. She'd talk to the wee thing in her belly like it could hear, talk about the plans she had for it, how it would have a better life than she'd had working alongside her daddy and brothers picking crops with the Mexicans.

Now the anger moved up through his gut and filled his eyes with outrage. These beaners, they not only thieved and destroyed, they infested the country with their filthy offspring until it would topple from the weight.

Ora picked up his rifle. Why'd this Mex woman have to be here now? Why'd she have to come at this moment? To face a gun in hand and anger boiling inside of him? Lousy trash, lousy piece of shit. That good-for-nothing wetback deserved this.

He walked back across the field to his porch, the hound at his heels, and sat down on the top step. He shivered as he laid the gun beside him and looked around at his farm. It wasn't much. A hundred acres, mostly juniper, scrub oak, and greasewood - and a lot of cactus. A line of cottonwood along the creek that was dry most of the year and one lone tree beside the house.

He looked at his hands, rough and broken from working this godforsaken land. Hell, he'd been warring with this farm for more than thirty-five years, trying to make the damn crops grow—keep the garden from wilting and hope there was enough water for the stock.

The house was old and needed paint. Porch rickety, windows loose so the wind whistled through them, playing a weird kind of music. The rest he kept as near as he could to the way Bea left it.

Christ, he remembered the day they found out about the cancer. They had to go to Tucson. The doc over in Douglas sent them. Ora felt like an outsider in that office. Bea did, too, he could tell. All those city people in their city clothes looking down on the two of them, him in his overalls, Bea in her old Sunday dress. They'd sat in that waiting room, sickness surrounding them. Ora had felt the huge weight of it, the weight of Bea's silent fear. And that little bastard who teased his sister right there in the office and made her carry on so bad with sick folks waiting there. Ora had to yell at the kid because his mother didn't know how, or wouldn't. And there was Bea sitting quiet, Bea who couldn't have kids anymore, who went through diabetes and stomach ailments and finally the cancer.

She'd been a tough woman. Married him after Nam, helped him save to buy this farm, consoled him when she was the sick one. She made life in this place seem worth the fight to keep it up.

Ora stared at the body lying out there by the brush. Bile rose in his throat. What the hell was he going to do? He could bury the woman. Nobody'd ever know. Who'd come looking for her?

Or he could cart the body over to state land. Let somebody find her. There was always some jackass, drunk and looking for sport, who'd use these scavengers for target practice—then go off and brag to his buddies. Nothing was ever done about it. Wasn't this just like Nam? Weren't you fighting for your life right here?

Finally, Ora got up. He took the rifle inside and propped it near the door, put on a work shirt, grabbed his old ball cap, and went back out to the chicken pen. A couple of the loose hens were trying to get back inside the fence. The others pecked around the ground in the distance. No use trying to catch them until they were ready, then he could lure them in with a little feed. He went on to the barn.

Bea had helped him build this barn. And she'd gotten some of the other farmers and ranchers around to join in. Ora would have kept to himself if it wasn't for Bea. She'd get back on her feet again after the hoppers ate the garden or the drought dried up the creek below the barn.

He'd buried her in that old Sunday dress. Looking down on her grave, he'd wished she'd taken him with her. He didn't think he could go on. But she'd told him when she was dying that he'd got to do it, got to keep up the farm for her sake, that she'd be watching up there and know if he wasn't pulling his part of the bargain. Some days he could hardly think, it hurt so bad. He wanted to just lie down and give up. To hell with it all. But then Bea would be there making him move on. He didn't know if she was really up there like she said. Didn't know if he believed in that. But she was in his head and that was bigger.

He went out to the garden. The heavy wire fence he'd put up to keep out jackrabbits and javelina had been cut and pulled back at one place, bent down from someone climbing it in another. The corn that was left was stripped and the pumpkin plants pulled up and tossed aside. Bea always loved the pumpkins - making pies and cakes and what all. He remembered the smell in the air of her cooking and his eyes got red and hot again.

"Goddamn you sons-a-bitches, ruining Bea's pumpkins," he yelled into the empty space. "By God, you deserve what ya get. Worse than the damn grasshoppers."

The hound bayed a response.

Ora fed the stock, milked the cows and put them all out to pasture, then did what he could with the fences, all the time that sick feeling inside, that anger, the hopelessness that ate away at him. When he was through, he walked back out to the brush where the Mexican woman lay. The sun was up by now and would grow hot in a few hours, baking the body on the ground mercilessly.

Ora squatted down to take a better look at the face. Young she was, young and serene in death. Hatred threatened to slip away as he looked but he grasped at it.

"Shouldn't-a looked at her," he hissed and jerked his head away. "Don't never look at the face."

Then in the quiet with the sun streaking down he heard a sigh - so small, almost not there. The chest of the woman moved and a hand twitched.

"Jesus, she's alive." And she was going to have a baby.

Ora's throat caught. Great welling tears filled his eyes, a cry almost like the baying of his hound, filled the air and he couldn't stop himself. He let all the misery spill out of him in huge gulping sobs. He sat on the ground, even after the tears subsided. Even as the sun rose higher ready to blast the earth with its heat.

Finally, his body and his pain spent and his decision made, he got to his feet. He bent down and lifted the young Mexican woman, blood from her right shoulder soaking his shirt. She weighed so little – just a girl – and carried her to the house, the hound and Bea following after him.

Present Enigma

Roger Antony

Mrs. Emma Hutchins, an 82-year-old widow, lived in a small cottage on the outskirts of Terra Verde, a small town in Yavapai County. She had one daughter and three grandchildren and doted over them whenever she could, but not so much recently because she had not been feeling well. She couldn't pinpoint an exact problem, although from time to time she experienced some dizziness and vertigo.

However, her malaise did not stop her from gardening, fixing delicious soups, and reading, but it raised alarms with her eldest granddaughter who offered to go grocery shopping for her weekly and pick up books for her at the local library.

Every Sunday afternoon for the past three months, Emma would call her eldest granddaughter and recite a list of grocery items she needed. Her call came precisely at 5:45 p.m. and lasted no more than ten minutes which gave Emma enough time to fix a cup of tea, turn on her television, and using her remote push the three buttons to bring up CBS's *60 Minutes.*

When her grandmother didn't call on Sunday by 5:50 p.m., the eldest granddaughter began to worry, but she let the worrying slide while she finished writing her article for the school newspaper.

It was not until the granddaughter's mother, Sidney Norton, asked what was on Emma's list that the eldest granddaughter became concerned.

Audrey Norton said, "She hasn't called."

"Call your grandmother. It's after 8," said Mrs. Norton.

Audrey put down her article, picked up her cell phone, and dialed her grandmother. There was no answer. "Should I drive over?"

Mrs. Norton looked at her daughter. "She may be in the bathroom. Call her in fifteen minutes. If she doesn't answer, we'll drive over."

Fifteen minutes later Audrey called, but again there was no answer. "Mom, I'll drive over."

"I should come," said her mother.

"It's only five miles. If I need you, I'll call."

"Take her house key. Call me as soon as you get there."

"I will," said Audrey grabbing a key to her mother's car from the hook on the wall next to the door leading to the garage.

Before Audrey shut the door her mother said, "Make sure you call me."

"I will," said Audreyletting the heavy metal door to the garage slam shut.

Fifteen minutes later Audrey was in Emma's narrow driveway. The interior house lights were on. That wasn't unusual. Her grandmother liked plenty of light inside when it was dark outside.

Audrey rapped loudly on her grandmother's door and shouted, "Grandma, it's Audrey."

Hearing no footsteps or verbal response, Audrey used her key, unlocked the door, and walked into the living room. In a louder voice, she repeated, "Grandma, it's Audrey. I'm here to take your food order." Hearing no reply, she detoured into her grandmother's bedroom, bathroom, kitchen, and back to the living room. Her grandmother was not in the house.

Audrey pulled out her cell phone and dialed her mother's number. "Grandma isn't in the house."

"Have you checked the backyard?" Sidney Norton asked.

"Not yet. I wanted to call you first."

"Call me after you check the backyard. Also, check the garage."

Audrey walked to the door leading to the garage. It was unlocked. She turned on the garage light, opened the door, and walked in. Her grandmother's car was there and the backdoor was ajar. Audrey opened it and walked into the backyard where she found her grandmother seated in an Adirondack chair, her head back, her eyes closed.

"Grandma, grandma," said Audrey touching her shoulder. Her grandmother didn't move so she repeated her words a bit louder and lightly shook her shoulder. Still, there was no movement or utterance.

Audrey put a finger to Emma's neck and felt for a pulse. There was a slight pulse. She debated for only a nanosecond who to call first, her mother, or 911.

Audrey stayed on the line with the 911 operator as questions were asked and answered. After hearing the ambulance sirens, she ran to the front yard to welcome the EMTs before calling her mother.

Sidney Norton sounded hysterical on the phone. “I’ll be right over.”

“Mom. Let dad drive.”

Emma Hutchins was taken to the Yavapai County Regional Hospital where she stayed in the ICU for observation before being transferred to the third-floor ward.

Audrey along with her younger sister, brother, and parents visited the hospital every day. While Emma was in the ICU, all they could do was stare through the glass. Beginning on day 3 when she was transferred to the third floor, they could talk and touch.

It was another 2 days before Sidney Norton drove her mother home from the hospital. Sidney called the high school and told them that Audrey would be missing class because of a family emergency. It wasn’t so much an emergency, as it was a family necessity.

When Emma Hutchins was comfortably settled in her own bed, her daughter went to the kitchen to heat some canned soup leaving Audrey behind at her bedside.

“Grandma, are you feeling okay?” asked Audrey.

“Much, much better,” she said, “Thanks to you.”

Audrey smiled as she held her grandmother’s hand.

“I have something for you,” said Emma pointing to her walk-in closet. “Would you mind getting it? I was going to give it to you as a high school graduation present, but I may not be around.”

“Grandma, you’ll be around.”

“Can’t be too sure,” said Emma Hutchins.

Audrey stood at the entrance to the closet waiting for instructions.

“You’ll need the step stool. There are three boxes on the top shelf. Each is marked. One’s for you, one’s for your sister, and one’s for your brother. Bring me the one with your name on it. Be careful, it may be heavy.”

Audrey looked at the shelf above her grandmother’s hanging clothes, but couldn’t see any boxes, but standing on the three-foot step stool, she could see three similarly sized boxes behind a cluster of leather handbags.

Audrey found the box with her name on it and as her grandmother had warned, it was heavy. Using both hands, she slid the box to the edge of the shelf then lifted it down and carried it to Emma's bed.

Emma looked at the containerboard box. "Thank you. I'm sorry it's not wrapped."

"That's okay. Do you want me to open it?" Audrey asked.

"If you can," said Emma smiling as she touched the box.

Audrey opened the taped flaps and withdrew an 8" x 8" x 8" metal box with a Master Lock style dial like the kind she used to lock her clothes in the women's locker room during swim team practice at the YMCA.

Audrey looked at her grandmother. "Do you have the combination?"

"I do somewhere, but I don't remember where."

"What's inside?"

"Something I hope you like," said her grandmother.

"So how do I open it?"

"You'll have to figure it out," she said with a smile. "Do you know how a dial lock works?"

"I do," said Audrey.

"This lock has four numbers. You turn the dial right then left, then right and left. If you have the correct numbers and sequence, the lock will open."

"Do you want me to look for the combination?" Audrey asked.

"Honey, I'm really tired. Could we talk after I take a nap?"

"Of course grandma," said Audrey. "Do you need anything?"

"No, I'm fine."

Audrey left the room and joined her mother in the kitchen where she was stirring canned soup in a pot on the range.

"Let grandma know we're about to eat. What's that?" asked Sidney looking at the small safe in Audrey's hands.

"Grandma wants to sleep," said Audrey then placed the safe down on the kitchen counter. "Grandma gave me this. She said it's my high school graduation present."

"You have two more years," said her mother.

"I know, but grandma says she might not be around then. She can't remember the combination, so it may take two years to figure it out."

Sidney Norton smiled. "It looks familiar. Your grandpa gave me a similar safe for my high school graduation."

"What was inside?" asked Audrey.

"Let's eat first," said her mother.

Sidney ladled soup from the pan into two bowls and walked them to the dining room. "As I recall, it took me almost a year to figure it out. I only figured it out after your grandpa gave me a clue."

"What kind of clue?"

"Have you learned about the periodic table of elements in school?"

"Yes."

Sidney Norton shook her head. "I shouldn't say anything more until I talk to your grandma. She may feel betrayed if I make it too easy for you."

That evening after serving Emma Hutchins dinner and watering her backyard garden, Audrey drove home with her mother in the passenger seat holding the small safe.

"Can you give me a clue?" asked Audrey.

"I talked with grandma. She said between you and your sister, you'll figure it out."

"You're kidding me."

"No, I'm not. Grandma thought I had already said too much."

"You mean about the periodic table?"

"Yes."

That evening Audrey showed Nicole, her younger sister, and her brother, Taylor, the small safe.

Taylor, only 7 years old asked, "How many numbers are required?"

"Grandma said 4 numbers."

Taylor reached over Audrey's arms and twisted the dial.

"Stop it, Taylor. Grandma said you turn the dial right, left, right, left and the safe will open."

Nicole said, "It's just like my lock at school. Unless you use the correct numbers in the correct order, it'll never open."

Audrey said, "Mom said that grandpa gave her a similar high school graduation present."

"Really, did she open it?" asked Nicole.

Audrey nodded.

The following evening Audrey had her science book out and was looking at the periodic table of elements. She was studying the table on the dining room table when Taylor sat down, looked at the periodic table, and said "What is this?"

Audrey said, "The periodic table. It shows the 118 chemical elements that have been discovered or made. It's arranged in the order of their atomic numbers."

Taylor shook his head. "What does that mean?"

"You'll find out when you take chemistry in high school," said Audrey.

Taylor moved his finger to the center of the periodic table. "What's this pointing to a box containing the symbol 'Au'?"

Audrey pointed to the opposite page where the full names of the elements were spelled out. "Au is the symbol for gold."

Nicole picked up the safe and shook it.

"Maybe there's gold inside," said Taylor.

"It's not that heavy," said Nicole.

"Well, there could be a coin or two," said Taylor.

Nicole studied the periodic table. After two minutes, she said, "Mom's first name is Sidney. The first two letters are 'Si'. It stands for silicon." She pointed to the table so Taylor could follow.

"So," said Audrey.

"Audrey starts with Au, which stands for gold."

"So what?" said Audrey.

"Does grandma know the combination?" Taylor asked.

Audrey shook her head. "She probably has the combination somewhere. She has a similar present for both of you," pointing to her brother and sister.

"Really?" said Taylor.

"Go talk to mom. Maybe she'll give you another clue," said Nicole.

"She gave me one clue - the periodic tables," said Audrey.

"If we can solve your combination, we'll be able to solve ours," said Nicole.

"Probably," said Audrey before leaving the table. "I'm going to bed."

The small safe remained in the center of the dining room table and every time Taylor passed by it, he turned the dial. Nicole did it less frequently. Audrey just looked at the safe as if touching it would give her cooties.

Two weeks later, while Audrey was driving home from visiting with her grandmother, Sidney asked, "How are you coming along on your writing assignment?"

Audrey responded, "About the same as figuring out the combination to the safe."

When Audrey was fully stopped at a traffic light, her mother said, "Do you want another clue?"

Audrey looked over at her mother then back at the overhead light. "What do you think?"

"I spoke with grandma this afternoon while you were watering her garden. She says that there's no reason you have to wait until graduation to open your present. Since you have a birthday coming up and she can't shop for your birthday present, she wants the safe to be your birthday present."

Audrey turned to her mother. "Does grandma want me to look through her drawers and cupboards to find the combination?"

"No, that won't be necessary."

"So, she gave you the combination?"

"No, but she gave me permission to give you another clue."

"I'm listening," said Audrey.

"How many letters are there in the alphabet?"

Audrey turned to her mother. "26, everyone knows that."

Sidney did not respond.

"Mom," said Audrey. The word uttered as both a plea and exasperation.

"You have everything you need to know to open the safe."

"Really," said Audrey.

"Your grandpa didn't give me this clue for months. In fact, every day of my senior year I thought about the combination. I thought it was cruel, but your grandpa didn't. He liked solving puzzles and anagrams and thought it taught one to think outside the box."

After dinner, Audrey sat alone at the dining room table with a sheet of paper torn from a notebook. She wrote 'Audrey' at the top of the sheet and below listed the two clues she had received: the periodic table of elements and how many letters in the alphabet.

She wrote out 'Au' then just below it, wrote the alphabet across a single line. When she was done she studied it. Nicole and Taylor joined her at the table and the three of them studied the two clues.

After a few minutes, Audrey got up from the table and said, "I'm going to bed," leaving Nicole and Taylor at the table looking at the clues and twisting the dial on the safe.

The solution to the safe conundrum came to Audrey at 4 o'clock the next morning, two hours before she normally woke on a school day. Fully awake, she rose from bed, padded down the hallway to the dining room, switched on the light above the dining room table illuminating the table, the chairs, the safe, and her notebook paper containing the two clues.

Sitting down at the table, she found her pen and was about to begin writing her solution when she noticed that the numbers 1 through 26 were already written below the letters of the alphabet. It looked like Nicole's handwriting. The sheet also contained a few pencil sketches of rainbows, houses, and trees.

Audrey circled the letters 'd', 'r', 'e', and 'y', and the numbers below: 4-18-5-25 then leaned forward and turned the dial on the safe's lock: right to 4, left to 18, right to 5 and left to 25. Her first attempt did not work, not because the numbers were incorrect, but because she was too excited and had not started the four-number sequence properly.

The second time was the charm and when the door on the small safe popped open she yelled loud enough for everyone in the house to hear and rush out of bed thinking the worst.

They found Audrey sitting at the dining room table with a smile on her face surrounded by a stack of photos, a twenty-dollar bill, and a gold ring on a gold chain.

Sidney Norton was not surprised to see the safe open or her daughter's excitement. She'd experienced the same excitement when she opened her safe. In her case, the numbers that opened the safe were 4-14-5-25 reflecting the last four letters of her name: d, n, e, and y.

After opening her safe, Sidney asked her father why the first clue had been the periodic table.

He said I needed a starting point, that I would quickly find'Si', the symbol for Silicon, deduce that my name was the key, and ultimately figure out that the four remaining letters in my name were the numbers needed to open the safe.

As she watched her children leave the dining room and go back to bed, Sidney Norton was certain that Audrey's sister and brother knew exactly how to determine the numbers needed to open their high school graduation safe.

Before falling asleep, Sidney made a mental note to talk with her mother about resetting the four numbers and revising the clues for the two remaining safes to ensure that both Nicole and Taylor had an enigma to solve.

Know When to Hold'em, Know Where to Toss'em

Carter Hale

The red and blue bar lights began flashing as soon as Ron tossed out a half-dozen beer cans.

"Oh, shit," said Neil.

We were in Neil's car. He was driving. Ron was in the front passenger seat and I was in the backseat.

Neil had decided we should discard our empty beer cans outside the main door leading to our high school gymnasium. He never said why, but since he was driving, we acquiesced and allowed our friend to make this unwise decision.

Earlier that night, we'd gone to a drive-in movie.

Back in the mid-sixties, there were several outdoor theaters in our area and that night they had a double feature. I don't recall the movie titles, but suffice to say they were probably second or third rate.

Before reaching the drive-in theater, Neil drove to Washington, D.C. where the drinking age was 18. A liquor store on Georgia Ave., just across the DC - Maryland line would sell to anyone as long as they could reach the top of the counter and paid cash.

That night Ron and I stayed in the car while Neil went inside and bought three six-packs of beer and several bags of chips. While both of us could reach the top of the counter, Neil felt the cashier might think he was making a straw purchase if we accompanied him.

We didn't disagree, so Neil, 18 years old and the only one in the car of legal age to buy alcohol in D.C., walked into the liquor store wearing loafers, pressed jeans, and a button-down shirt.

He might have been mistaken for 19, but he certainly didn't look 21, the legal drinking age in Maryland.

Ron and I waited patiently in the car and smiled with delight when Neil emerged from the store with two brown paper bags containing food and drink.

We arrived at the drive-in theater just before dark. After Neil parked his faded green 1959 Plymouth next to a speaker post, Ron grabbed the speaker and placed it on the door, turned it on, and discovered the volume control adjusted the speaker static from low to high.

We talked about moving to another location to find a better speaker, but by the time we agreed to move, the drive-in was full.

We hoped that the cars on either side would have blond cheerleaders, but there were no cheerleaders, only young men like ourselves.

We spent a good portion of the evening talking about school, girls, and college while the movie played and the speaker squawked.

Each of us had been accepted into college and would matriculate in September. Neil would not be joining Ron and me at the University of Maryland in College Park. He had been accepted at Western Maryland College, now called McDaniel College, in Westminster, MD.

Despite living most of my 17 years in Maryland, I'd never heard of Western Maryland College or Westminster.

I thought Neil was lucky to have parents who could afford the tuition, room, and board for four years at a private college.

It was well before the end of the second film when we mutually decided that staying another hour or more would be a waste of time even though there was beer left.

After Ron returned the speaker to a hook on the post, Neil started the engine and drove slowly away.

I didn't question Neil's sobriety or his ability to drive even though he had likely consumed a six-pack.

The drive to my house took nearly forty-five minutes. As he approached my house I said, "I'll take the empties and put them in our trash." I even said that my father would have no objections to filling up one of our multiple trashcans with the detritus of the evening. Instead of stopping and letting me out and allowing me to discard the empty beer cans in our trashcans, Neil drove past my house, turned the corner, and headed out of my neighborhood without saying a word.

My next thought was that he wanted to take Ron home first because he wanted to talk to me about a private matter. Instead of taking the road to Ron's house, Neil turned left then thirty seconds later made a right turn into our former high school.

I wondered why we were visiting our high school at two o'clock in the morning, but in less than a minute it all became clear as he slowed his Plymouth to a crawl and drove around to the main exterior entrance to the gymnasium, stopped at the curb and turned off his headlights.

It was pitch black. There were no lights on inside or outside the gymnasium or on the other side of the roadway: the athletic field and track.

"Why are we stopping here?" I asked.

"Let's dump the trash," Neil said.

I said, "When you drop me off, I'll throw the trash in our trash cans."

"Chuck it here," said Neil.

I don't think Ron cared what we did with the trash so he opened his door and started offloading the trash into the concrete gutter, 20 feet from the main entrance to our high school gymnasium.

Ron was still pushing trash out of the car when a hundred feet away a set of headlights turned on spotlighting us as the red and blue bar lights on the top of a police car began flashing.

We stared into the headlights and saw one police car and two officers. One policeman exited and slowly approached us.

If it happened today, I'm fairly confident that the officer would have called for backup and approached us holding a Glock automatic, but times were different then. He held a metal case for letter-size paper.

The police officer's slow walk from his patrol car probably took only ten seconds, but it felt like eternity.

As the officer approached, Neil tightened his grip on the steering wheel, shook his head in disgust, and told us that his father, an attorney, would be really pissed having won a major case in court the previous day.

I too was embarrassed by our actions and didn't want my parents to hear about this.

Upon reaching the driver's side door, the police officer shined his flashlight into our faces and asked for our driver's licenses, then asked if we knew we had broken the law.

We produced our driver's licenses, apologized for our actions, and stated that we knew that littering was wrong.

The police officer showed no emotion during our collective statements of contrition.

We watched him return to his patrol car with our licenses wondering what actions he would take and what punishment we could expect for our wrongdoing.

I also wondered if this infraction would go on my permanent record and if it would jeopardize my college matriculation in less than two months.

While we waited for the police officer's return, we discussed our stupidity.

Although I was in the car and technically an accomplice to the littering, I was neither the driver nor the one who pushed the trash to the curb. Feeling somewhat innocent, I said, "You should have let me put the trash in our cans."

There was no disagreement from either Neil or Ron.

Our anxiety continued to rise as we waited for the officer to return.

Fifteen minutes later the police officer walked to Neil's door and handed back our driver's licenses, one at a time while shining the beam of his flashlight in our faces. He gave us a very brief description of our misconduct, told us never to litter again, to pick up the beer cans and chip bags and leave.

Ron quickly opened his door and retrieved all of the trash he'd pushed out. When Ron finished cleaning up the mess, the police car turned off the flashing bar lights, backed up, turned the corner, and drove out of sight.

Neil started his car and drove slowly in the same direction as the police car while Ron and I stared out the Plymouth's windows. We didn't see the police car while exiting the high school property, but it wouldn't surprise me if the officers had stopped, turned off their lights, and watched us depart.

Neil drove Ron home, then me. He didn't take me up on stowing the trash in our trash cans, so I'm not sure what he did with the beer cans and empty chip bags, but I suspect he found somewhere to legally dispose of the trash before arriving home.

Top Box

Linda Foote

Life's journey is a mysterious thing. At age seventy-two, I never expected to travel down a road of discovery—only to find myself...

It started with the ding-dong of the doorbell and signing for the certified FedEx package addressed to me: Susan N. Fields, 36 Indian Trail, Denton, New Hampshire. With a return address of Hyde, Hyde, & Saunders, I had mixed emotions about opening the large, official-looking envelope. What is this? Someone suing me? Being audited? No, that would be the IRS. Maybe I won the Lucky Dog sweepstakes I entered online?? After undoing the sticky flap, I withdrew its contents. Inside were documents from my deceased aunt's estate. Page two read: One Sarah N. Wells, nee Grove, of 407 Park Street, Westfield, MA, leaves to her niece, Sandra N. Fields, nee Stewart, Plot #311, Berkshire County, town of East Everett, MA, including all structures and contents thereon.

"Is this for real?" I asked. "There's a lot of legalese jargon. It says there are 2.8 acres with a summer house and an outbuilding." I handed the packet to my husband, a retired business lawyer. "I remember meeting your aunt at your mother's funeral. She was your mother's sister, as I recall. That was what...over forty years ago?" "Yes. Aunt Sarah spent lots of time at our house when I was growing up. She rented an apartment, two streets over from us. I always thought she didn't have much money." "Let's have a look." He went to his desk and pulled out the rest of the papers. Standing behind him, I tried to stay calm. I counted forty-eight-floor tiles, and twenty-seven law books before he finally spoke.

"Yes, these are official. There's full disclosure here—no liens or back taxes. You'll have to make an appointment and provide the attorneys with proof of identity. There are instructions on this last page." Removing his glasses, he looked up and grinned. "Well, my dear. Once you sign the papers, looks like you'll be the owner of property in western Massachusetts."

I was shocked. After my mother passed, soon after I was married, I'd lost touch with Aunt Sarah. I assumed she had died years ago. According to the documents, Aunt Sarah never married and lived to be ninety-one. An enclosed map showed that the land was located in a very rural area. What shape was it in? What am I going to do with another house at my age?

Aunt Sarah was a year older than my mother, and the last time I saw her was at my mother's funeral. They were not only sisters but best friends. I knew when Aunt Sarah was visiting: the strong aroma of perked coffee, and clatter of spoons on our mix-n- match china. I can picture them sitting at our kitchen table, chatting for hours. Often they would talk and giggle between good-to-the-last-drop re-fills.

As a child, I never understood their conversations. Once I asked, "Aunt Sarah, why don't you have any babies?" My mother gave me one of her stern glares, but Aunt Sarah chuckled and said "Little Susie, God didn't want me to have any. Guess you'll have to be my baby." Other times, when I asked what they were talking about, my mother would say: "It's grownup talk. You'll understand when you're a grown-up. Now go play."

They exchanged birthday gifts and sent each other greeting cards for special occasions. Every celebration we had included Aunt Sarah. Until my graduation from high school, she would proudly present me with a special gift at the end of each school year—canned bath powder or a little plastic tube of the latest Avon lotion. Until I turned twenty-one, she never forgot my birthday.

I remember going to her apartment and seeing piles of colored cloth surrounding her black Singer sewing machine. She was always working on a project. One year she made me a stuffed Mother Goose for Christmas. It was white with large orange stitches and a big yellow beak. Another time, she crocheted blue booties for everyone in the family. I remember, for my fifteenth teenth birthday, she made me a flowered shawl with long, red fringe. I only wore it when my mother made me—I was embarrassed to wear it around my friends.

Quite often I'd stay overnight with Aunt Sarah. She'd help me put on lipstick and we'd go to Friendly's for ice-cream suppers. In the evenings we'd play "Old Maid" or "Crazy Eights." I remember that she was always fun. She was the only lady I knew who dyed her own hair, wore bright red lipstick, and gobs of makeup. When I was eight, I remember she dyed my hair red; my mother was not pleased.

~

At the attorney's office, I spoke with Pauline Hyde. "Is there any way I can see the property before taking ownership? What if I don't want it?" "Mrs. Fields, your aunt left specific instructions in her will: one being, you're not allowed on the property until you sign these papers. There are other stipulations as well. This property is to be yours, and yours alone. Lastly, there's to be no financial hardship to you at transfer of ownership. This includes all taxes and utilities." "Utilities? I don't understand. Isn't that unusual?"

"Yes, highly unusual. However, specific arrangements have been made to have bills automatically paid, 'in perpetuity.'" "What? How is that even possible?" I asked, trying to grasp what she was saying. "I had no idea my aunt had that kind of money."

"I'm sorry, but I can't divulge any other information, due to attorney-client privilege," Pauline stated. "Sign here and we'll process the transfer of title. Expect four to six weeks before receiving the deed."

Praying this was the right decision, I took a deep breath, crossed myself, and signed. "Here you are, Mrs. Fields," Pauline said with a smile, handing me a packet with my signed documents. "It's been a pleasure working with you. Congratulations."

~

The next day, my husband and I drove to inspect the property. My emotions were all over the place—excited, anxious, then worried. Would we find a gem or a joke? The place was hard to find, even with the help of GPS. Once in the town of East Everett, we were directed through several turns and down a desolate rural road. Tall, budding limbs of oaks and maples reached over the narrow lane. At first, we drove past the tree-shrouded entrance, not realizing it was a driveway. Turning around, my husband parked on the roadside, not getting too close to potentially side-scraping shrubs.

"This must be it. Let's take a look," I said, swallowing my disappointment. "Doesn't look too promising." We picked our way through overgrown brush and followed faint tire tracks up the dirt drive. It led to a stone walkway and a small yellow house. I smiled and gave a big sigh.

"I was worried that this was all a hoax. Isn't this beautiful? Like something out of a picture book," I said.

"From this distance, maybe. Looks like a lot of work to me. But, yeah, guess I can see the potential," my practical husband replied. "But I'm reserving judgment until we do a thorough inspection."

A map of the property showed the general layout. We found an old wire fence along the back section and located several stakes marking the east boundary line. We walked around the outside of the house, circa 1930, including its detached shed. The cottage was nestled on a grassy clearing surrounded by tall maples and pines. Branches of a huge lilac bush overflowed into the front porch. "Let's see what's it's like inside," I said, clutching the key. It slid in easily, and the lock clicked open. Holding my breath, I opened the door. Stale, dusty air greeted us. To our delight, the lights flicked on. "I'll check the water," my husband volunteered, heading to the kitchen. "The attorney was right," he announced a few minutes later. "Both electricity and water are working. I bet the gas is hooked up, too."

While he investigated, I stood in the living room, taking it all in. The picture window overlooking the front yard, the wide-pine floors, faded wallpaper with pink roses, and wood beams across the ceiling were flooding my senses.

"Yes, gas, too. It's all working and the meters are running," he said returning from the outside.

"That's great, honey," I said. "But did you notice all these dust covers? This place is furnished! Pauline never mentioned that. What a nice surprise!"

We walked through the house, unveiling items: an overstuffed yellow-flowered couch, two lounge chairs, a dinette set. Each of the two bedrooms had a double bed, a bureau, and a bedside table with a lamp. The bathroom was small but equipped with a vanity, tub, and shower.

"Definitely a diamond-in-the-rough," my husband quipped. "The driveway needs clearing and yard needs work."

"But in here, I can do the work myself," I reasoned.

It sounds selfish, but this is the first time in my life that I've owned something that's totally all mine. I've saved a little money and was wondering what to do with it. All it needs is a couple of cans of paint, some elbow grease, and I'd call it Home! A sense of peace engulfed me. I felt I belonged.

The following week, I packed my Camry with clothes and food for several days. I included candles and a bottle of wine—to celebrate my first overnight trip.

"You sure you don't want me to go with you?" my husband asked, carrying out my suitcase.

"No. I need to do this myself. I'll be fine. This is a great adventure for me!" I gave him a hug and kiss.

"I'll call you when I get there."

It took three hours to drive to East Everett. This small New England town had seen better days. I passed The Merrill Paper Company, whose doors closed in the early '70s. Windows were broken and piles of colored pulp sat along the riverbank. After crossing the bridge, the tiny town square appeared with its white gazebo. A cluster of small cookie-cutter homes lined both sides of the street. My turn-off was just ahead. I had not bothered using the GPS—I didn't need the help. I remembered each turn as if I've been driving this route for years. I clearly saw the opening that we missed during the first visit. Much to my surprise, as I entered the driveway, it was now well pruned and void of tree limbs and overgrowth! I stopped the car and stared. How could this be? I called my husband.

"You won't believe this. I was able to drive right up to the house. The driveway is all clear. The brush is all trimmed back. I'm looking at a manicured lawn and newly painted house!"

Was this all for me? How beautiful.

"Did you know work was being done? Did you authorize any of that?" my husband asked. "I suggest you call the attorneys before going inside. Hopefully, they'll know what's going on."

I immediately call Hyde, Hyde, & Saunders. Much to my relief, Pauline was there and explained:

"The refurbishing of the property was specified in the will. Once you signed papers, we were instructed to make it move-in ready. I hope the updates and changes are satisfactory. If there is anything else needed, please let us know."

"Yes, thank you, thank you..." my voice drifted off.

I was amazed at the extent of my aunt's foresight. Inside, the house looked much the same, except clean and tidy. I was astonished.

The rest of the dust covers had been removed and furniture arranged. The windows had been washed and the floors were newly polished. There were towels on the bathroom shelf and new linens in the closet.

I opened the kitchen drawer to find a new set of silverware. Two new cherry-red pot holders were stuck to the side of the refrigerator with magnets. As I unpacked the car, it felt like the house was welcoming me home.

On the wall above the dinette set hung a pretty oil painting of fruit in a bowl. I noticed it was the only picture in the entire house. It looked like the hanger had come loose. As I went to adjust it, it broke and the picture fell into my hands. I flipped it over and found a tiny key, with a small wad of paper, taped to the back.

Curious, I carefully removed them. The key felt warm in my hand. The piece of yellow-lined paper had been folded several times into a rectangle. I smoothed it out and read:

"For Little Susie. Look for Top Box." I gasped. Aunt Sarah, is this from you? How did you know I would be the one to find this? What does it mean? I plopped into the nearest overstuffed chair and I closely examined the key and the note.

My mind was racing as fast as my pulse. The note was hand-written in red ink. Is this Aunt Sarah's handwriting? I can't remember. But who else would use "Little Susie." her pet name for me? Is there a Top

Box somewhere that opens with a key? A jewelry box? Hidden drawer? Maybe Aunt Sarah had a safe deposit box somewhere.

I inhaled deeply, placed the items on the table, and stood with a determination I didn't know I had.

I methodically searched the living room, kitchen, and bedrooms for anything that might be a Top Box. I found nothing. Maybe whatever belonged to the key had long disappeared. I wandered outside to clear my head. It was a warm, late spring afternoon. I looked over the backwoods and stopped a moment to breathe in the wonderful air. This felt so right—totally in balance, and peaceful. A cardinal sang and other birds joined in. I'll buy a bird feeder and plant some flowers. Maybe there are some gardening tools in the shed. A piece of plywood acted as a ramp. I tried the handle; it didn't move. The house key in my pocket fit and I pushed open the door. It was dark inside; it took a minute for my eyes to adjust. Straight ahead, neatly piled containers were stacked against the wall. I saw a toolbox and a lawnmower. I turned around. Steel shelves held numerous boxes of different shapes and sizes. Each was labeled with black marker: Summer Clothes, Party Favors, Yarn, Dishes, Cotton Cloth.

Then I sensed it more than saw it—a gray strongbox with rusted corners. It sat by itself on the top shelf. I stood on tip-toes. With trembling fingers, I carefully took it down. I tried lifting the lid. It was locked. Top Box. I had nearly talked myself into thinking it didn't exist, yet—here it was.

After staring at the box for several minutes, I carried it into the house. I picked up the tiny key and placed it in the lock. It turned easily on the first try, with a gentle click. What did you want me to discover, Aunt Sarah? Will I finally have my questions answered? Taking a deep breath, I summoned all my inner strength, and slowly lifted the lid. I lifted out a brown leather-bound book, the sole contents of Top Box. A journal? A diary?

I took the book into the living room and turned on the side lamp. The shadows were growing longer and dusk was settling in. I prepared a cup of hot peach tea, put on my reading glasses, and curled up with a blanket on the faded couch. I opened the cover: the first few sheets had been torn out of the book, but on the page facing me was a handwritten letter dated fifteen years earlier.

Dear Susan,

Please forgive a selfish and foolish old man for his ramblings but I must make this confession to ease my own conscience before I leave this earth. These secrets have been heavy on my mind and heart for over fifty years. I hope you will forgive me for what I am about to reveal. Your Aunt Sarah came to me out of desperation. She wanted a divorce from her husband, Jack Harding, who was abusing her under the guise of marriage. Divorce was scandalous and nearly impossible for a woman to initiate. I was a young lawyer and had opened my own practice. After hearing her dreadful story, I consented to take her case. She was beautiful, sophisticated, courageous, and nineteen. I was twenty-nine, successful, married, and fell madly in love with her.

Sarah knew from the beginning that I had a wife and child but said she didn't care. She loved me and I loved her, that's all that mattered. We spent many wonderful weekends in this cabin, away from prying eyes and nosy family. Sarah loved this house and she loved me. I admit I took advantage of her. She was young, needing security and love, and I gladly provided it. Lies and deception came easily. I used her, needed her, and I loved her. I kept my family and firm far away from us. I remember the day she came to me with the news she was going to have a baby. She was so excited to tell me. We were deeply in love by that time. I'm so sorry, forgive me. I did not take it well, I'm so sorry.

I placed the book in my lap and took a sip of tea. I tried to take in what I just read. My mother and I lived alone, my father having died long before I could remember. But I never knew my aunt had been married, then divorced. And she was pregnant? This was a young Aunt Sarah, one I never knew. I looked around the room. She and her lover had spent time here, keeping their affair secret from the world. Even after all this time, I could feel her uniqueness: the faded couch, the flowered wall-paper, and the boxes of sewing materials I'd found in the shed.

Who was this man and why was he writing a letter to me? What happened with the baby? I picked up the book, eager to find out more.

I was unwilling to take responsibility. She was a free spirit and I was a married man. It broke my heart when she left the cabin, our special place. But I could not keep her, or the baby. Sarah was my world, but I'm so sorry I did these terrible things to protect myself and to protect her from scandal. I had seen it again and again in courts—how single young women with a child were treated. She spoke so often of her dear sister; they were so close. It was almost too easy, going to her sister and convincing her to claim the baby as her own. Don't blame Sarah. She was vulnerable. I convinced her that what we were doing was best for the baby. For you. I had access to hospital records, legal documents, and plenty of money. I used my position to legalize names on the birth certificate. By devious means and bribery, I was able to keep our secrets. I kept my reputation pure on the surface while delving deeper and deeper into layers of deception—and time passed. That is why, after all these years, I have kept this house in her name. I couldn't let go of the only place and time I was truly happy. I have loved her with all my heart and soul throughout my life. Please, my daughter, do not judge me too harshly, but I'll understand if you cannot forgive.

Your Loving Father,

James Hyde, Sr.

The founding father of Hyde, Hyde, & Saunders? I read the letter, over and over, stunned. Aunt Sarah, can this be true? My world had been turned up-side-down.

On the next page was the last entry:

My Little Susie,

Reading this, you have taken possession of the house and have found your father's letter. Discovering that I am your biological mother, and James Hyde is your father, must be a shock. Your mother never exposed us and took our secret to her grave. Out of love, we did what we thought best for you. Despite the deceitful things he did, James is the only man I ever loved. I know he loved you, in his own way. I gave you up to the person I loved the most, your mother. Don't blame her. I insisted. Mothering was not in me. She raised you as her own. I was able to visit you and be in your life, without regrets. Your mother and I always had a special bond, and sharing you between us was pure joy. We often thought about telling you the truth, but the time never seemed right. Your mother and I were always proud of you and thrilled when you married. When she died, a part of me died. Seeing you reminded me of her; I could not bear it. Knowing you were well cared for and happy, I needed to getaway. I was surprised to learn that James bought our special place, and left it to me. I found the box. I read the letter he left for you. He wrote me a letter, too. I carry it with me to this day. It gives me great pleasure to know he loved me to the end. While staying here summers, I embraced the memories. My health is waning, and this is my last visit. In his letter to me, he left instructions to pass this property on to you. Whenever you arrive, I hope you'll find as much peace and joy here, as I have. You'll always be my Little Susie.

Your Loving Mother,

Aunt Sarah

Tears streamed down my face as I gently closed the book. Emotionally battered, yet, I felt surprisingly whole. Confused, betrayed, angry, but blessed and loved. Was I a changed person now that I know the truth? Does it even matter?

I thought about giving my husband a call, but decided to wait until morning. I needed time to process. He might want to investigate, get the truth out. I decided to keep this secret to myself, at least for a while. Smiling, I took out the candles and wine. What better time to celebrate? Candles lit, I arranged the book, box, and key on the table. Taking a sip, I sighed. Thank you, Aunt Sarah, for bringing me home.

The Transport

Greg Picard

It was a long drive from Cuyamaca State Park down to the County Jail in San Diego. Ranger Chris Becker didn't have to make too many arrests that required jailing a person, but it came up more often than he liked, especially due to the extended transport time. Inevitably, like now, it was late, and he would not get home until the Witching Hours. His daughter would have to fend for herself for dinner. She was halfway to a Bachelor's Degree, so he figured she could for sure handle dinner, but still, it made him feel bad as a single father to be absent so much because of his job and its weird hours.

This particular incident took the better part of the afternoon and evening to deal with by the time they found the perpetrator and managed to talk him out of the tree...fifty feet up. They might never have found him if he hadn't still had the red ball cap on. It was his first dumb mistake in the chase. Chris figured he was so used to wearing it he didn't even think about it being there.

His second mistake was trying to overpower Becker when he stepped down finally from the tree. The wrestling match wasn't pretty, and Chris got thumped pretty well by the larger man. He had at least fifty pounds on the ranger. He finally got a good hold on him and thought he'd be able to cuff him when the guy somehow came up with Chris' pistol. The wrestling match over that was even more epic, but Chris managed to push the magazine release, and it dropped into the mud. Without the magazine, the gun wouldn't fire, even with one in the chamber. So his quarry tried to clobber him with the butt. Fortunately, Chris finally got him in a chokehold from behind and rendered him unconscious long enough to cuff him and retrieve his weapon and clip.

"You're a pain in the ass; you know that?" Chris yelled. "And you're stupid. Now on top of everything, you've got an assault against an officer charge." He angrily pushed him, stumbling toward the Azalea Trail that led to his Bronco in the campground.

His name was Clark Azemadian. It sounded like such a respectable name...one an accountant or a manager at Safeway should have. This guy was far from that. The beard was down to his chest. The hair on his head was in a foot-long ponytail. The tattoos were so many that his natural white skin was almost invisible. Most of them were X-Rated or just plain angry expressions of hate. The only one that was out of character was the one of "Mother." It was the traditional heart with an arrow through it. Chris thought it uncharacteristically sweet until he found out the man had shot his mother with an arrow. Fortunately for her, she survived, but the relationship apparently didn't, and the event was memorialized by him on his arm for some bizarre and demented reason.

That's how Becker thought of the man. Demented. He took extra care when he secured him in the back seat of his Bronco.

He drove the winding twists through the backcountry on highway 79 until it emerged at an onramp to Interstate 8 southbound. Neither one of them had had food for the last ten hours, and Chris was hungry. He didn't see how he could avoid giving the man something to eat if he stopped for food himself on his way down the highway.

"I suspect you're hungry?"

"I could eat my Momma right now, I'm so hungry."

Well, that was disgusting," Chris said, as his appetite took a dive on the thought.

"I'm gonna stop for a burger at McDonald's, if you want one and can behave."

"Sure, no problem."

Chris had his doubts. This man had been nothing but problems. He planned to keep the man in the back seat and toss in a burger. He had locked his prisoner's feet in a chain to the floor's eye hook when they started the trip. He now switched the man's hands in the cuffs to be in front of him so he could manhandle the burger. It was risky, but his feet were locked down, and he'd still keep him locked behind the barrier screen in the backseat compartment, which had no window or door release handles on the inside of the doors for him to use to get out.

He went through the drive-through window at the golden arches and then parked with their food in the lot. He would have preferred parking off a bit more alone, but the lot was packed with cars, and it surprised him at this late hour even though it was a Saturday night. This Mickey D's must have achieved 'hangout' status with the teen crowd. They were everywhere. He wedged himself between two cars into the only space left, and it was so narrow that he suspected he wouldn't be able to exit the vehicle if he had to. He rolled down both windows on the front doors to feel the cool night air. It had been a hot summer in the mountains in more ways than one. He'd been working on a prescribed burn plan, dealing with a bumper crop of visitors, and trying to avoid a boss he didn't get along with as much as possible.

The car on his left was filled with teenage boys laughing and throwing out curses words to punctuate every sentence. Two of them closest looked over at Chris and his charge in the back seat.

"Hey, look! The park fuzz has a prisoner. Hey fatso, what'd you do, steal a pine cone?"

The rest of the morons in the car thought that was hilarious for some reason. Chris ignored them and rolled the window on his side back up accompanied by a chorus of giggles from the teens.

So what's it like bein' a ranger?" his prisoner asked.

"Probably not much different than any other job," Mr. Azemadian.

"Call me Azzy, everybody does. Your job sounds like a good gig. Workin' in the woods."

Chris wondered about the nickname. How many times was he mockingly called 'Ass' instead? As big as he was and with his propensity to use his fists, perhaps not often. Still, he bet it happened, even if it was behind his back.

It was an hour's drive to the jail. Chris wasn't much into making friends with people he arrested, but he was going to be stuck with this one it seemed for a while, so he asked, "What's with all the tattoos?"

"You don't like 'em?" Azz frowned.

"I think most folks would find a lot of them pretty offensive, but to me, it was more a question of why so many?"

"Yeah, kinda is a lot, I guess. My Mom hated me to have a tattoo, so I got more just to piss her off. You could say, we didn't much get along most of the time."

"What did your father think of them?"

"Never got to really know my father. He disappeared by the time I was two. I hardly remember the bastard."

"So what's the deal with your wife? Why beat on her?"

"She kept whining about how her mobile home burned down."

"Why would you beat her for that."

"She reminds me of my mother."

"That's your reason?"

"She blames me."

"For what, the fire?"

"Yeah."

"And just why is that?" Chris felt like he was pulling teeth getting information from this guy.

"No good reason."

"I think you're leaving something out."

"Well, I was pissed at her like usual, and she was pissed at me, and I took my six-pack outside to drink it in peace. I got to thinkin' about how the place was insured, and we'd be better off with the money. I had my eye on this really cherry Camaro. The place was a dump. So I guess I kinda set fire to it."

"Kinda?"

"I tossed one of my butts, and it accidentally landed on the gas can for the lawnmower."

"Let me guess; you didn't have the cap on it."

"She'd started bitchin' at me about what a crappy job I did on the lawn when I was filling the damn tank on the mower. I got distracted."

"That's the tale you told the cops, that it was an accident?"

"Yeah."

"No wonder." Chris didn't know what else to say. No surprise, they had a warrant out for him. And why was his wife still with him, he wondered?

"So, does your wife know that's how the fire started?"

"Not exactly."

"Not exactly? What does that mean?"

His prisoner didn't answer.

It was a special kind of stupid that did things that way. The conversation had reminded him that this guy was crazy and just edgy enough to have more warrants for his arrest. He had been so involved in searching for him and taking him into custody on the wife-beating charge, that he hadn't run him for other wants and warrants. He clicked his radio mic between mouthfuls of his double cheese and requested a 10-29 through dispatch from CLETS and NCIC.

A minute later, the results came back from dispatch, showing a warrant for arson in Oklahoma. He hung up the dash mic as a woman, and a girl about five wedged alongside his Bronco to unlock their door. The child was intrigued by Becker's police vehicle and turned to his prisoner in the back.

"Are you in jail, mister?" she asked.

"Not yet, little missy. The park ranger thinks I should be, though."

"Did you do something bad?"

"I climbed up one of his trees." He laughed.

Her eyes got wide. "I'd like to climb trees," she said as her mother lifted her into the back seat. "Someday, my Daddy is going to come back and take me to climb trees!" It was then that Chris noticed the brace on her leg. It reminded him of people he'd seen suffering from polio, and he wondered if that was her issue as well. Polio was an unheard-of problem these days as far as he knew."

"Would you like one of my cookies," she said as she leaned back out the open door and extended one toward the small space in the Bronco's rolled down rear window. Becker was about to intervene and shoo her away when Thompson reached up with his cuffed hands, and Becker pushed the control to lower the rear window very slightly more so his prisoner could take the cookie. Azz smiled broadly, showing his missing front tooth. "Thanks," he whispered. Chris thought he detected a catch in his voice as the man said it.

"So you kinda maybe possibly accidentally set fire to her mobile home in Oklahoma?"

"Yeah, kinda."

"You know there's a warrant for your arrest for that?"

"Yeah, bitch told 'em we'd been fighting, and I probably did it on purpose. They believed her."

"Wow, Imagine that." Chris laughed. "And just how have you managed to keep from being arrested for it? Dispatch said it happened almost a year ago."

"It's Oklahoma for shit's sake."

"That's supposed to explain it to me?"

"There's, like, maybe one cop per county. More Cows than people. 'Sides, I didn't stay put there. I worked a rig in Texas for a while until she found out where I was and said she wanted to get back together...did I mention she sorta kicked me out of her burned up single-wide?"

"Just *before* you took your six-pack and then burned the trailer, I'm guessing?"

"Well kinda, yeah."

The little cookie girl was finally secured firmly in the adjacent car and had rolled down her window. She leaned out and handed Azz another cookie. "You look, sad, mister. Cookies can fix sad real good!" She smiled. Her mother seemed increasingly uneasy and must've hit the power window button because the child's window slid slowly up as she leaned back into her seat and continued to look at Azz.

It suddenly struck Becker that the kid had no father figure in the car, and he wondered if the woman was single, and the girl looked for a Daddy in every man she met. She could certainly do far better than this sleaze, he thought.

What was even stranger still was that as Chris looked into his rearview mirror and saw Azz in the backseat, he noticed the man had a tear rolling down his cheek, and he was awkwardly trying to wipe it away with his cuffed hands. Chris wondered, was it the little girl and her kindness? Azz likely was deficient in those kinds of experiences for sure or was he finally grieving the mess he'd made of his life and the future he likely faced now. The punks in the car on the other side weren't helping with their catcalls and slurs. He considered asking why he was crying but decided it was his prisoner's private hell to deal with, and there was little he could do to change things. Frankly, he wondered if he wanted to, even if he could.

He crumpled his burger wrapper into the ashtray and cranked over the engine, and as he pulled out of the space, he noticed Azz flip the teens off and then turn to the little girl and wave goodbye to her smile.

What Really Happened

D. D. Mazur

Imagine a seahorse.

More precisely, rather think of a seahorse lookalike; visualize its gigantic and weird cousin, about five and a half feet tall, who despite its large size, appears equally fragile as its tiny relative. Its head is strikingly similar to the seahorses we know, and a rugged, elongated straw-like snout ending with a small, round mouth with spikes instead of teeth, renders the critter its characteristic, horse-like appearance.

The beast had no eyes, and being blind didn't seem to bother it much, while the crown on its head, a coronet, was substantially larger than one found on an ordinary seahorse. Add to it a flexible neck and thin, iridescent skin covered in tiny hairs stretched over bony plates, with changing skin colors according to the angle from which it is observed, alternating from deep purple and red, to green and turquoise blue, with a dozen bony plates arranged in rings around the body, and a dozen more around the tail.

Most seahorses have prehensile tails and use them to balance and maintain their bodies in a vertical position floating in the water or wrap them around underwater plants or corals to help them remain stationary. The ones I'm describing, however, had the tip of their tails firmly buried into the ground, inciting a question of whether the creatures actually belong to the animal or plant kingdom.

This was challenging to determine: these forms were feeding on live insects and other creatures, which they swallowed whole through their mouths, but also made energy through photosynthesis the way plants do, using chlorophyll pigments interspersed across their skin.

The seahorses known to us are fish, although not fish-like, but are uniquely designed; nevertheless, possessing all the characteristics, which make fish fish.

Seahorses live underwater, breathing through gills, and have a swim bladder. The species I am describing had none of these fishy properties, quite to the contrary: no trace of them in seas or oceans, they thrived breathing air under the open sky and survived living on flat terrains, attached to a soil bed rich with minerals and nutrients, sprinkled with rocks and boulders mixed with wild grasses and bushes, an occasional tree.

The field they occupied also included strange-looking bulges accompanied with curious objects of various shapes and sizes, seemingly randomly scattered around, with two common features: they were all attached to the ground, and they all appeared organic.

The seahorse look-a-likes would sway gently in the air, following the breeze, loving the sun's rays, slowly chasing after the sun's daily journey through the sky.

They seemed fragile, which wasn't deceiving, as they depended on weather conditions. Their living area had to be blessed with a mild climate, spared from high winds, and severe climatic conditions because strong air movement could damage their delicate tails, even break them, and knock them to the ground. If that happened, their life ended.

There was only one place where they existed in their comfortable, open meadow. From the north, the uphill sloping Central Mountain provided wind protection, and to the south dense forest furnished a shield. Between the forest and their habitat, a gentle stream of water was encircling the terrain, so impeccable it was doubtful if the creek was built intentionally as a canal or a natural creation.

In either case, this landscape provided almost ideal conditions, and the environment was suitable for their flourishing, procuring good fortune for many years.

I could never tell whether the creatures were part of the animal or plant kingdom. Their seahorse-like appearance clued their relationship to the world of fauna, yet, unable to see, and rooted in the ground they couldn't go places, begetting them members of the plant kingdom, for I heard of few animal species deprived of the ability to change location, and I know of no animal having roots and chlorophyll.

Their gender distinction was impossible to say, perhaps because it was unimportant, but they were endowed with another trait of utmost importance, one I was very clearly made aware of.

Wearing only their own skin covered in tiny hairs, producing chlorophyll to convert light into energy, and feeding on raw food caught through secretion of a chemical with a flower resembling fragrance, they also possessed stunningly developed intellectual comprehension. Its magnitude and nature were way above my ability to assimilate and understand it. Their highly advanced acumen followed a very different path than humans, but savored marvelous capabilities, and was of proportions and levels of achievements beyond my most audacious imagination.

They transpired thousands of years ago, on this piece of land, found on a semitropical island, which they inhabited peacefully for centuries, but exactly how they evolved remains unanswered.

I call them 'Zaons,' short for 'Zaldistatsons,' because this perplexing word was somehow the closest interpretation of how I've seen them in my mind's eye.

There were many thousands of Zaon individuals inhabiting their range, with their social structure different than ours: it was more similar to a colony of ants. They acted as one single, collective organism, mysteriously interconnected despite the lack of physical contact with each other. The entire colony functioned and behaved as one single, unique entity.

* * * * *

Zaons were not the only inhabitants of the island. They shared it with a brilliant, progressive human race, the Zaons 'recognized' as 'Beshte Bathozuix.' Zaons 'called' the island 'Lurrayhartecco', but I should stick with the more familiar name, Atlantis, and its human dwellers, Atlanteans.

As a young man, I'd read a bit of Greek mythology, and learned a little about the myths and legends of Greeks, Romans, and Egyptians. The Atlantis fable was somewhat familiar to me, as was the Greek philosopher Plato, who first wrote about it.

I'd never given much thought about Atlantis, but being skeptical in nature, I stashed the story in the same folder where Santa Claus was kept. Highly doubtful, but you never know.

What I learned through my encounter with SPI - short for sand, pebbles, and Indal - forced me to rethink my assessment about Atlantis. I am well aware that folks even less skeptical than myself might continue questioning the authenticity and reality of it. Because I can't offer anything more than my words, I am prepared not to hold grudges against cynics out there. For me, however, the legend became supported by other realms from my past and present life, and despite being peculiar and inconceivable, I had no choice but to accept it as factual. This ended my debate on whether Atlantis ever existed or was only the product of someone's imagination.

Anyhow, these bizarre revelations had become a permanent part of my memory, embedded in me during my first and only session with SPI, and as curious as they sounded; I accepted them as truthful, having no proofs or indications to the contrary.

The Atlanteans occupied a large part of the island, living peaceful, prosperous lives, and enjoying a pleasant, mild climate; the environment stimulated opulence and prosperity. It was the land of plenty. The soil was rich with nutrients and minerals and combined with gentle weather allowed for two harvests per year, supporting an abundance of plant and animal life.

The people of Atlantis were organized as a monarchy, divided into sections, ruled by kings, who were close relatives, descendants of the same wealthy family, speaking the same language, and living in harmony next to each other.

On the contrary, Zaons were only one single dominion, located on a comparatively small, middle section of the island, in the valley where the slopes of the Central Mountain began, rejoicing in their peaceful meadow. They stayed there for many decades; maybe centuries, secluded, hidden from Atlanteans who avoided the Central Mountain believing it was where gods resided.

The only visitors were occasional large animals, mostly bears, who became lost browsing in their field, sometimes damaging a few Zaons, before being driven away by the odor Zaons secreted to protect themselves from such nuisances.

Although having very limited abilities in manipulating space, Zaons were not completely helpless.

But everything changed when humans arrived.

Their very first encounter with humans was a good one. Many years ago, a young single man discovered the Zaons' territory. He didn't believe gods would object to his presence and he preferred living outside his own society. He settled at the edge of the Zaons range, living in the small wooden cabin he built. He was a gentle man whom I will call Lotron, in honor of my favorite childhood book. He would pay occasional visits to the Zaons field, fascinated by the changing colors of their skins. He thought Zaons were guardians of gods' mountain residences and sensed that they were more than plants or animals. Although he couldn't figure them out, he respected them and never did anything harmful to 'gods guards.'

In time, Lotron married and had three boys. He would sporadically show and allow boys to play in the Zaons field, teaching them to respect and not to harm things found in the field.

As the boys grew up, they became curious about life outside their limited world and started exploring, eventually moving to the village, and, to Lotron's regret, integrating into Atlantean society. They became successful sailors and traders, connecting with a world outside the island. They sailed all over the Mediterranean Sea and visited places and tribes surrounding it.

When Lotron died of old age, it was only a matter of time before Zaons would encounter other people.

Lotron's sons' childhood stories about the existence of a field of unusual 'gods guarding' creatures on their own island got their close attention. According to Lotron's sons' explanation, if you didn't try to pass the field of guards and approach the mountain, the guards would do you no harm.

The Atlanteans were curious people by nature, and fascinated by the world they traded goods with and dreamt of conquering it. Knowing that there was a portion of their own island still Terra incognita was too much of a challenge. No longer fearing the gods' anger, they organized a small expedition of explorers and sent them to survey the place.

*****

This was how the Zaons country was discovered. The explorers were captivated by the unusual, colorful appearance of the seahorse-like plants, and their slow movements under the summer breeze. They were unable to identify Zaons as non-human species of intelligent life.

Although the explorers had no ill intentions toward their new discovery, their presence soon became harmful to Zaons; thinking of them as plants, people started picking them, as if they were flowers, and using hatchets to cut them down. This was equal to slaughter.

Humans attempted to collect and bring samples of their discovery back home, but the Zaons, cut off from their roots would rapidly decay and decompose, and many were destroyed. People then started digging them out from the soil and placing them into big vases, attempting to keep them alive, but with many accidents and failures in the process, the Zaons population was dwindling.

Zaons were unable to avoid the fast-moving humans, who threatened their existence, causing terror within their community. They couldn't know if and when the intruding men would end the destruction, which was crippling their colony.

Unable to respond to the situation with the speed needed to address the danger, fear spread amongst Zaons. Despite having limited abilities to respond, the Zaons were not completely defenseless, only slow.

Zaons had the ability to produce different fields, called 'systozas,' without using mechanical devices, which humans had never encountered before: a quantitative physical phenomenon, such as electric, magnetic, gravitational, acoustic, and other fields. These fields couldn't be detected or perceived with ordinary methods, even though they were physical realities, occupying space, creating specific conditions in it, and containing energy. The systoza fields could come in various types and ranges.

Zaons could achieve unusual outcomes with different fields. They could create acoustic waves of frequency and intensity sufficient to cause earthquakes. I recalled Nikola Tesla's claims that he had discovered ways to make earthquakes, wondering if his knowledge somehow originated from Zaons.

On this occasion, Zaons started releasing small, but powerful systoza fields, the invisible balls of sound pockets, which floated in the air near them, spreading around in a breeze, waiting for the opportunity to enter someone's ear.

Once inside the head, the sound pocket would unwrap and start exploring the host's mind to determine damaging bio-resonance in the victim's brain. The frequency, wavelength, period, and amplitude differed from person to person, but the systoza had the ability to identify each individual's specific, harmful resonance, and formulate a series of harmonics, which would be released in the victim's head. The infected person would 'hear' it either as a melodic segment similar to earworm, voices, or noise, or whatever sound combination capable of inflicting audible attack.

The sounds would graduate according to individual compulsive preferences, becoming louder and more annoying with time, and in a matter of minutes would incapacitate the infected listener, who couldn't get rid of the annoyance, leading to permanent insanity, literally driving them crazy and opting for suicide as the only solution to escape the 'voices' in their heads.

The Zaons strategy worked all too well on the intruders. When systozas began creeping into people's heads, they aborted their destructive behavior toward Zaons and started frantically running around, pressing their hands against their heads, screaming, and yelling in utter horror.

Of the seven explorers, one man was pulling his hair, jumping up and down, loudly groaning in pain and terror, while another two were banging their heads against rocks until falling down and fainting, covered in blood, and subsequently dying. Two men attacked each other, hitting each other with their fists until one pulled his sword, and slaughtered his opponent, then driving the machete into his own torso, falling to the ground, jerking as if exposed to electric shocks.

One Atlantean who was heavier than the other explorers, suddenly spontaneously combusted, bursting into flames, screaming and running toward the water in a nearby stream, but before reaching it, collapsing on the ground, rolling in the dirt but failing to extinguish the flames which were consuming him.

The scene panicked the last man, who seemed otherwise unaffected by the attack, but was beside himself, exposed to this horrific happening, not understanding what was going on. He ran away from the field of death and was the only one who survived this bloody defense of the Zaons.

The survivor's name was Rion, and he escaped thanks to the fact that he was almost completely deaf. His ear canals were closed shut, and systoza was unable to enter his head. It was sheer luck to escape the systoza 'infection,' and he ran away like mad, as the petrified witness to the demise of his colleagues.

It took Rion five days to return to his civilization, and during that time he didn't eat or drink. His clothes were tattered, and his face and hands were dirty. He looked like a ghost, scaring children who first saw him, as they ran away screaming and yelling in fear.

Rion was asked to report the event to the King himself. Although deaf, he could talk and described the horrific event in the only way he knew how, with mystical interpretations, garnishing his story with details from his vivid imagination, full of fear, magical explanations, and supernatural speculations.

Zaons were frightened, predicting humans would come back, retaliate, invade their world and destroy their future. The consequence could be catastrophic for Zaons and could end with their eradication.

To protect themselves, they managed to release in the stream encircling their field an invisible wall of systozas, an acoustic defense mechanism, set up to 'ignite' sound pockets on approaching intruders, repeating the earlier tactics of entering the ears of unsuspecting listeners, and causing them to go crazy.

In the meantime, the King decided to check the Rion's saga, and directed a strong military unit, a battalion of one hundred soldiers, to research and determine the truth behind the only surviving explorer's story.

They went, but their mission ended in tragedy: they were defeated the same way as the first group of explorers, most of them dying under circumstances similar to the first occasion.

Zaons victory came with a hefty price, because the soldiers set the colony on fire, and slaughtered great numbers of helpless creatures with swords before the defense mechanism of Zaons began showing their deadly effects.

A few soldiers survived, and returned home, confirming Rion's story. They added their own interpretations and described seeing and hearing the lethal sirens, strange creatures living in the water, singing irresistible tunes. Some described sirens as beautiful half-naked girls, and some like terrifying looking monsters. The secret of Zaons defense system was uncovered: it was the acoustical weapon, which they were using so effectively.

The Atlanteans were outraged and looking for revenge. Figuring out what caused their debacle, they felt encouraged and empowered to retaliate and achieve final victory.

The King, who was at the beginning curious and careful, became angry, his anger turning to hate. He concluded that victory was within reach, planning on the elimination of the threat.

His fury was fueled by the loss of his men, and he asked his relatives, other Kings, to join him in defense of their society from, what he described, a threat to the entire island.

A coalition was formed, and a huge army was assembled, determined to eradicate the hazard. Their strategy was to cover their ears with wax, which would disable the penetrating capacity of the enemy, and proceed with burning and slaughter. What fire wouldn't destroy, the swords would.

They were right. No soldier was harmed by systoza sound. Few Zaons left unharmed after the attack realized that their systoza defense system wasn't working.

The remaining Zaons put in place a different line of defense. They created a large systoza field, which probed the land and released a powerful, low-frequency infrasound, silent for people but devastating for the earth. The land started vibrating and moving, shaking, and splitting. It gradually increased in intensity and wouldn't stop. It was a massive, strong, and long-lasting earthquake. Zaons hoped it would interrupt superstitious humans in their attacks. Indeed. But the earthquake was the most powerful and strongest ever. The shaking continued, as the island was resting on the South Atlantic Ridge, and the fault at the bottom of the ocean also started to move, resonated by the initial earthquake, opening a gap in the seabed, and causing a chain reaction. The fault shifted creating a huge rift and abyss in the bottom of the ocean, directly underneath Atlantis, and the land above it began to collapse, flattening the fields and mountains, valleys, and hills. Everything from above was sinking under the water. It was a total cataclysm: the massive shifting of the earth's core continued, swallowed people and Zaons, trees and streams, turned the land upside down, drowned everything, violently sending the entire island under the sea. The agony lasted through the night and the ocean swallowed the entire island in a disastrous event, which later found its way into legend, described as God's punishment for human greed for power.

After it was over, only ocean water with floating debris could be seen covering the area where Atlantis had been, while the island crashed on the bottom of the sea, with all its residents drowned.

After a while, the debris was flushed away by the ocean currents, and only myths and legends about Atlantis were left.

Polio

Pat Fogarty

In the early summer of 1954, the Polio Virus invaded my Bronx neighborhood.

As a 4-year old, I clearly remember getting struck with polio before the vaccine came out.

The image of my mother standing over me with a worried look on her face and massaging my arms and legs with rubbing alcohol will be with me forever. Mom's friend, Jamie Davey, a neighbor who lived on the floor below was with her.

Later in life, I learned that my mom's friend Jamie, like my mom, were both World War II, U.S. Navy Veterans.

I have an unshakeable memory of being 100% paralyzed on the entire left side of my body. I could not move my left arm or my left leg. And I could barely turn my head.

The next thing I recall is seeing two men in white talking to my mom. At the time, I did not know who they were or what was going to happen next.

We lived in a three-bedroom apartment in the Highbridge Projects on the seventh floor. There were 117 apartments in the 13-story building.

The two men in white placed me on a gurney and strapped me so I could hardly move. They rolled my crippled little body from our apartment down the hallway and into the building's elevator. At that point, all I remember is that my mom was not with me. I was scared.

When we got to the first floor there was a crowd of onlookers in the lobby. It was deathly quiet and everyone was staring at me.

As the two ambulance attendants guided the stretcher out of the building, all the people moved back away from the gurney

It was dark outside and the ambulance was parked in front of our building. A police car with its Cherry-Red emergency light was lit and spinning alongside the ambulance. Both vehicles were parked near where the Good Humor Ice-Cream Man would setup his Ice-cream cart in the daytime.

As my young paralyzed body was being placed in the back of the ambulance, I saw my older sister Kathy strapped into the only stretcher in the vehicle. She could talk. I couldn't.

The muscles controlling my vocal cords were affected by my new sickness.

In 1954, most ambulances were just oversized station wagons fitted with a variety of emergency medical supplies.

When I was hit with the polio-virus, many New York City Hospitals used converted Cadillac Station Wagons as ambulances.

Today ambulances are larger and far better medically equipped than they were in the 1950s. However, Funeral Parlors still use the same type of converted Cadillac station wagons to transport the deceased.

When the ambulance attendants began moving my body from the gurney to place me in the stretcher alongside my sister, I recall trying to tell the attendant that I couldn't breathe. He must have understood my garble because he turned my head so that I could get air.

My sister and I were strapped together like Siamese twins on the sole stretcher and taken to Willard-Parker Hospital.

Willard-Parker was a communicable disease hospital located on East 16th Street in Lower Manhattan along the East River. It was founded by the City of New York for Infectious Diseases in 1885.

Thankfully, in 1954 Willard-Parker Hospital was way ahead of the curve with an amazing but controversial method of treating polio patients.

Nearly eighty-five percent of the pre-adolescence polio victims treated at Willard-Parker recovered and most suffered little or no obvious signs of ever having polio.

Willard-Parker Hospital used the *Sister Kenny Method* for treating the afflicted. The Sister Kenny Method included; completely wrapping patients in damp steaming wool blankets, using heat packs on the affected muscles, and careful persistent exercise.

Looking back, today many medical experts attribute Sister Kenny's method of treating polio patients as the beginning of a new field of medicine we now call rehabilitation medicine.

In 1954, Dr. Salk's polio vaccine was tested in a placebo-controlled trial, which enrolled 1.6 million children in Canada, Finland, and the United States.

Out of precaution, no one from heavily populated areas, such as New York City, took part in the test.

In April 1955, Salk's vaccine was adopted throughout the United States. *(By that time, I had been released from the newly opened New York University Rehabilitation Center.)*

Although Willard-Parker Hospital was overwhelmingly successful for treating and curing polio victims, it was looked down upon by most other American Hospitals for its use of the unconventional Sister Kenny Method of treating polio.

After all, Sister Elizabeth Kenny was a self-trained Australian bush nurse who developed a new approach for treating victims of poliomyelitis, which was extremely controversial at the time.

Along with the hot damp blanket treatment, I would spend several hours a day in an Iron Lung.

As Kathy and I regained use of our muscles we were transferred to the NYU Medical Center at 34th street, also on the east side of Manhattan. Kathy's stay was a short one. Her recovery was much quicker than mine.

My Sister's room was across the hall from mine. And, as Kathy was being released, I went nuts.

Although we were not in the same room at the NYU Medical Center, the nurses made sure we had daily contact.

By the time my 5-year-old sister was being discharged, I, as a 4-year-old, was strong enough to hold onto the tall crib rails and stand; something most children can do at 10 months.

And just to add on to the memory of the day Kathy was discharged, I remember after she left, they let me have her room. The room she vacated looked over the FDR Drive and getting her room meant I could see the East River with the boats and barges traveling up and down the river.

I also remember seeing the huge gas tanks on the Queen's County side of the East River.

Today, besides being a little claustrophobic from being wrapped tight in those hot damp wool blankets, every-time I go into our hot-tub in our backyard, I am reminded of the stainless-steel shallow tub with powerful water jets they put me in during my rehabilitation at NYU.

I know I can't possibly thank the Doctors, Nurses, and Staff who worked at these hospitals 66 years ago. But I do thank God, especially every time I see someone in a wheelchair.

Writing about my polio experience and the vaccines kids got in the mid-1950s and 60s triggered many forgotten memories.

I also remember the feeling of helplessness as I was wrapped like a cocoon in those hot-damp blankets.

Plus, I will never forget the times spent in an Iron-Lung. Nor will I ever forget; not being able to shoo a fly away from my face with my arms strapped inside the compression chamber of the Iron Lung with just my head sticking out of the beastly contraption.

As I became more mobile, I remember a day came when the hospital staff put me and several other polio victims into wheelchairs and loaded us onto a special bus.

The *Barnum & Bailey Circus* had come to New York's Madison Square Garden and the people running the circus gave free tickets to all the New York area hospitals. Madison Square Garden set aside a special section with wheelchair access for all the kids the hospitals brought to see the Circus.

I recall the colorful clowns handing out free flashlight-twirlers to each kid in a wheelchair. That was my first trip to the Circus. And years later when I went to the Circus for the second time in my life as a young adult in the 1970s, the memory of being in a wheelchair & being wheeled in to see the Circus in 1954 came right back to me.

Today, I occasionally still have a flash-back to my bout with polio.

A few weeks ago, I needed to have an MRI done for an upcoming surgical procedure on my knee.

I was told to lay flat on my back and to keep perfectly still on the platform that draws your body into the belly of the MRI machine.

When the MRI machine started, and my body was being moved by the machine into the tube for the MRI, my nose started to itch. That's when; once again the memory of being in an Iron Lung was triggered.

Thankfully I only had to manage the itch for a few minutes. Whereas, when I was getting treatment in an Iron Lung, I often had to lie there for a few hours before the hospital staff removed me from the Iron Lung and I could scratch the itch.

By the Grace of God and Sister Kenny, with her method for treating Polio victims; I have lived a life without really being hindered by my bout with Polio.

At the New York University Medical Center, I received the finest polio rehabilitation care on the face of the earth.

I remember the encouragement and prodding I would get on a daily basis. A marvelous team of physical therapists worked with me every day. Learning to walk and talk again was a difficult challenge for a four-year-old.

I remember waiting in line with other young polio victims to walk across a platform with hand railings to hold onto to help support our legs. We each had our turn to try to get across the walkway with the support of the handrails. One of the therapists would be in front of the child and one was behind the child as we each attempted to complete the task.

Besides working in large groups for certain physical therapy exercises, we also receive plenty of one on one care with daily muscle massages and muscle resistance exercises.

Of all the therapy given to me at the NYU Medical Rehabilitation Center, the most vivid memory I have is of the speech therapy I received.

Not being able to verbally converse with others, caused me as a four-year-old an extreme amount of frustration. The speech therapy I received at the NYU Rehabilitation Center seared my mind with a slew of un-erasable memories.

I vividly recall several of these painfully frustrating sessions. One that continued to play over and over again in my mind for years involved a male therapist who became very angry at me when he was unable to get me to say the word he wanted me to say.

In 1954 the speech therapy room at the New York University Medical Rehabilitation Center had a window with a clear view of the Empire State Building. This particular therapist had me sit at a table near the window and would show me cards with various pictures on them. I'm sure it was all simple stuff like, cars, boats, trucks, and other such items a 4-year-old could verbally identify. When I finished identifying and pronouncing the names of all the pictures on the cards, the therapist pointed out the window at the tall building and said "What's that?"

I tried to say, a cloud and when I said it, I clearly remember him speaking to me in a loud voice.

Once again he pointed out the window towards, what I know now, was the Empire State Building and he said, "What is it?"

Again, I tried to say, "a cloud".

The man raised his voice and said, "A Clown? That's not a clown! What is it?"

I was four-years-old sitting in a speech therapy room with an angry man who could not understand my words. I remember my frustration at him not realizing I was trying to say cloud, not clown.

Looking back now, I don't even think he noticed the clouds in the sky. I think he was too focused on the famous building and could not fathom why he thought I was seeing a *clown* and not a tall building.

I have no idea what I may have been thinking back then, but I do know my experience with that particular speech therapist embedded itself in my memory.

When I was finally released from the hospital they sent me home with a set of leg-braces and a pair of crutches.

The braces were the first to go, followed quickly by the crutches. I never made it to kindergarten but by the time I was 6 years old and entered the first grade of grammar school, I showed no physical signs of ever having polio. My legs were strong and although I never won any track medals, I played most sports fairly well.

I was one of the lucky ones. Several other children in my Bronx neighborhood caught the virus in 1954 when it swept through New York City. Sadly, many who contracted the virus were sent to other area hospitals that did not use the Sister Kenny Method to treat polio. Most of those unfortunate victims never recovered.

I remember one kid in particular. His name was Barry and he lived in the same building as I did. We both got the virus the same week in 1954 but were taken to different hospitals.

When Barry was released a few weeks after me, they sent him home in a wheelchair. His legs were totally paralyzed and even though we remained friends, I always felt a little strange seeing him in the wheelchair.

About a year after Barry returned home to the Highbridge Projects, my wheelchair-bound friend and family moved out of the neighborhood. As the years passed by, I realized more and more, just how lucky my sister and I were to have been taken to Willard Parker Hospital.

Although it has been close to 70 years since I was wheeled out of my Bronx apartment on a stretcher, I still have one affliction to remind me of my bout with polio.

Three years ago, while having my thyroid examined by an Endocrinologist, the doctor was a bit startled when he scoped my throat to have a good look at my thyroid.

The doctor asked me if I knew my left vocal cord was paralyzed.

I told him that I did not, and then I told the doctor about having polio as a child.

It was at that point that the doctor started telling me how lucky I was. He said that if the left vocal cord was not 100% paralyzed in the exact spot it was; that I would not have been able to speak at all.

The Endocrinologist went on to explain; in order for a person's vocal cord to create a sound, one vocal cord must be able to touch the other as we speak.

He then said, "Pat, the only reason you can speak is that your left vocal cord is paralyzed in the exact spot it needs to be for you to make a sound."

Learning that my left vocal cord was paralyzed helped me understand some of the challenges I have faced over the years. I remember back in the late 1950s when I tried to sing along with Elvis on the radio and how disappointed I was when my dear mom who normally encouraged me to try, and try again, said to me, "Patrick, give it up, no matter how hard you try, you'll never be able to carry a tune, not even in a bucket."

*A typical Polio Ward before Polio Vaccine became available in 1955

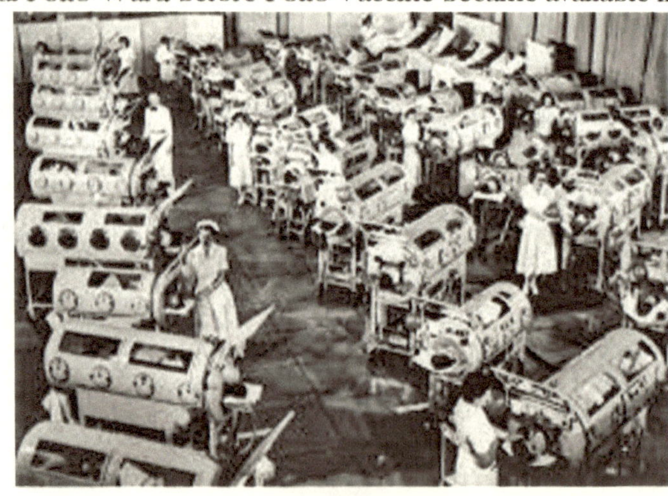

Why Didn't They Believe Me?

Cordell Compton

August 1901

"Who is the little guy waiting in the hall near the Chief's office?"

"I don't know," said John Ashton, the Chief's secretary. "I figured you might have a clue. I'll say one thing, though: he's a patient man. He arrived after lunch and has not moved."

"Any notion what he wants or where he's from?" inquired Mark Williamson, Assistant Chief.

"I have no idea why he's here. However, he's from New York City and a cop. He showed me his badge. It has blue and gold embedded in it, so the guy is no ordinary flatfoot. His appointment was at 1:30 pm. Guess the Chief is running late for some reason, although he is normally on time."

Williamson and Ashton stared at the compact gentleman sitting in an armchair about fifteen feet away. The visitor looked more like a bank clerk or schoolteacher than a law enforcement officer: small frame, pinstriped suit, bowtie, high-collared shirt. The bowler hat in his lap completed the clerk's "uniform."

Finally, Ashton walked toward the patient gentleman who stood holding his hat and looked hopeful. "I am sorry, Sir, about the wait. Usually, Mr. Wilkie is on time for his appointments, but not today. Can I get you a glass of water, a cup of coffee, maybe a cigar?" Ashton shifted his weight from foot to foot and feigned a cough as he looked at the small man in front of him.

The visitor's dark eyes narrowed to slits while he sized up Ashton. "No, thank you. I'll be all right. I'll continue to wait for Mr. Wilkie." Relieved, Ashton nodded and scampered down the hall to his office with Williamson. *I wouldn't want to meet that guy in a dark alley.*

More than one person had that identical thought rumble through his mind. That was especially true if he were on the wrong side of the law. Giuseppe, or Joseph, Petrosino emigrated to America from Italy as a young teenager with his family and siblings. They settled in the Little Italy section of Manhattan. Joseph eventually learned English.

By good fortune, he landed a street sweeper's position that involved pushing a cart through the streets, shoveling up trash and horse manure day after day. In a quirk of the organization chart, the Sanitation Department came under the jurisdiction of the New York City Police Department. Petrosino was pleased that his job helped his family survive in a new country. He was a steady, vigorous worker.

Eventually, the young man caught the eye of a sympathetic police officer who vouched for him when Joseph applied for a job in the Department. When he became a twenty-three-year-old New York City Police Officer in 1883, Petrosino proudly wore Badge #285. The downside of Joseph's accomplishment was threats against him made by members of his neighborhood where police officers dealt with mistrust and suspicion from citizens whom they were sworn to protect.

Petrosino applied himself as an officer with the same diligence as when he swept New York City streets. His language ability was an asset to the Department when he investigated crimes and issues involving members of the Italian community.

Again, his persistence, drive, and motivation caught the attention of Police Commissioner Theodore Roosevelt, who promoted him to Detective Sergeant in charge of the Homicide Division in 1895.

None of that mattered now. Petrosino opened the lid of his pocket watch and snapped it shut. He closed his eyes and rested his head against the wall behind the chair. His patience trickled away by the second. *Almost two o'clock, been waiting for over an hour.*

Momentarily, Joseph heard a commotion at the opposite end of the hall. Someone stomped up the stairs. He saw a well-dressed man disappear into Ashton's office. Ashton then popped out of his office and hurried toward Petrosino.

"I apologize again for the delay, Sir. Mr. Wilkie has returned and will see you now. Please follow me."

Petrosino silently rose and accompanied Ashton to Wilkie's private office. Ashton could feel Petrosino's stare penetrating his back as though they were bullets.

Wilkie walked from behind his desk and warmly greeted Petrosino. He towered over Joseph by nearly eight or ten inches. "Please have a seat, Mr. Petrosino, although I suspect you're tired of sitting. I apologize for delaying our appointment.

"I was on my way back from the Treasury Department when a presidential staff member stopped me on Pennsylvania Avenue in front of the White House. He said the president needed to see me, so I couldn't refuse that request."

"I see," replied Petrosino, "I understand how these things happen." His impatience lessened with each breath upon learning the cause of the delay.

Wilkie leaned back in his chair and lit a cigar. He blew out the match, took a few puffs, then swiveled around to face Petrosino.

"Commission Murphy's telegram has puzzled me since it arrived several days ago. So, what 'matter of extreme importance' does a New York City detective sergeant have that would interest the United States Secret Service?"

Petrosino's eyes bored more holes into Secret Service Chief John Wilkie. "I would consider the safety of President McKinley of 'utmost importance' wouldn't you?"

Wilkie's eyes widened while he puffed on his cigar. He knocked ashes into the ashtray and rested the stogie on the tray holder. The office filled with blue smoke.

"Yes, I would consider the president's safety of 'utmost importance.' What are you talking about, Mr. Petrosino?" asked Wilkie. "What information do you have and where did you get it?"

Wilkie was trying to decide into which category Petrosino fitted best: crackpot, braggart, blowhard, or genuine informer.

"Mr. Wilkie, the information I collected several days ago was in the normal course of my duties."

John Wilkie raised his hand to pause Joseph's narrative. "What exactly *are* your duties?"

"Six years ago, Mr. Roosevelt promoted me to Detective Sergeant in charge of the Department's Homicide Division."

Wilkie raised his hand again. "You mean Mr. Roosevelt, the vice president?"

"Yes, I do.

"I suspect you know in a city of our size, crime is prevalent. There are many homicides, and my unit investigates those cases. For example, there were over four hundred homicide arrests two years ago.

"In the course of those investigations, we discovered the existence of a secretive criminal network operating in the city. This network, or syndicate, operates illegal gambling houses, prostitution rings; they intimidate merchants and shopkeepers who must pay 'protection' money to stay in business.

"It is tough to arrest anyone connected with this outfit. Any potential witnesses to these activities will not testify for their safety. They tend to have 'poor memories' when it comes to remembering details or recognizing faces. Amnesia is a persistent disease in some regions of the city.'"

"Go on," said Wilkie.

"While we were investigating some murders in my old neighborhood, we uncovered a few anarchist-types mixed up with this organization. During our questioning of these guys, we found disturbing information."

Wilkie leaned forward in his chair; he relit his cigar and puffed several more times to keep it going. "Continue."

"Based on what we uncovered, we heard these anarchists were actively plotting to kill Mr. McKinley."

"I see. Do you have any details about this 'plot' such as dates, time, location, methods, individuals involved? Anything like that?"

Joseph Petrosino fingered the brim of his hat. He looked at the floor for a moment, then at Wilkie. "No, Sir, we don't have any solid information to pass along. I wish we did. I felt it was my duty, however, to notify you and your agency in any event. Advance information like this could have prevented the assassinations of Mr. Lincoln, and President Garfield had it been discovered and reported."

"Yes," replied Wilkie, "information like that would have been important back then. But it may not have made any difference in those days. You see, what protection we give the president is spotty and unofficial."

"What do you mean 'unofficial?'"

"It's straightforward, Mr. Petrosino. The Secret Service has no statutory authority to protect the president. When we try to give him any protection or guards, he often shoos us away. Remember, politicians like to mingle with the voters who elect them. Anything or anyone who gets in the way is not welcome."

"That's different from what I thought," said Petrosino.

"It's what we in the Service have to live with every day. And few people know our limits. We have to concentrate on our original mission: catch counterfeiters and protect the United States currency," responded Wilkie.

"So, you couldn't increase your 'unofficial protection?'"

"No, not without more credible information regarding a threat."

Petrosino's frame seemed to contract as he sat in front of Wilkie's desk. He fingered his hat brim again and peered out the window behind Wilkie. "Is there *anything* you can do, Mr. Wilkie?"

John Wilkie leaned back in his chair, took several puffs, and set down his cigar. "Before you leave, give whatever information you have to Mr. Ashton, my secretary. I'll pass it along to our New York City field office. Maybe they can turn up something. Thank you for coming to see me."

Wilkie stood, shook hands, and wished Petrosino a pleasant trip back to New York City. He sat down, scratched his chin, and reflected on their chat. *Interesting little fellow. There's probably nothing to his story. Yet, what if?*

September 6, 1901

Several weeks later, Petrosino walked along East 57th Street in Manhattan on his way to a nearby precinct station. He paused at the 2nd Avenue intersection for traffic to clear. A newspaper vendor hawked a special late-afternoon edition on the corner.

"Extra, Extra," shouted the lad. "Read all about it. President McKinley shot in Buffalo, New York."

Petrosino bought a copy to read the front-page story.

Why didn't they believe me?

Just One More

James Downey

Corporal Dane Hansen watched helplessly as the lead Huey helicopter in his formation exploded in mid-air, killing everyone aboard. The barrage of Viet Cong Rocket-Propelled Grenades that had appeared from nowhere began to take out other helicopters to his right and left. Dane was crammed sardine-like into his Huey, tightly packed with Army combat infantry troops awaiting their order to jump to ground into the rice paddy below. They were next. Dane crouched at the open side door, first to jump, an impotent spectator to his death. He leaned out the doorway and retched.

Withering machine-gun and automatic rifle fire from the dense jungle surrounding the rice paddy raked the formation. Although Dane was still too high in the air to safely jump, he hurled himself out the door as a stream of machine-gun rounds stitched its way across the side of the helicopter towards him, tearing into those who seconds earlier were directly behind him. The deep muck cushioned a landing that would have otherwise broken his legs.

Dane dropped to his knees to absorb the impact, continuing to fall face down into steaming water buffalo dung. He could only lay there, pinned down by the heavy field pack on his back. One nostril submerged under a fist-sized water-filled depression. He gagged and tried to hold his breath. Instead, his rapid, labored gasps for air sucked water into his nose and mouth, effectively waterboarding himself. A wave of panic engulfed him.

The unending firestorm raging inches above his head ripped his pack to shreds. Each round felt like it had hit his body. He wept and shook uncontrollably. A mortar round exploded, raining debris and shrapnel on top of him. Something heavy and metallic fell hard on his head. As he faded into blackness, his dying scream joined the chorus around him.

Dane felt a gentle hand touch his shoulder and heard a soft female voice whisper in his ear. Was this an angel, welcoming him home to heaven?

"Dane, wake up, it's all right. You're safe, you're home." A soothing arm drew him closer. He slowly opened his eyes. His shaking and sobbing were real. They hadn't been part of his dream. His wife of twenty years, Brenda, his only reason for living, had quietly and lovingly endured another one of his nightmare flashbacks to his Vietnam combat days. He was tied up in the covers and drenched with sweat. It was 6:30 a.m.

Ashamed, confused, angry, and overwhelmingly grateful for Brenda's faithful love, Dane pulled himself out of bed, crawled through the shower in a daze, and stumbled into the kitchen. He poured a cup of cold, sludgy coffee leftover from the previous morning and headed to the living room to watch the sunrise over his rural hometown of Gilbert, Nebraska. Years ago, coffee had replaced whiskey and drugs as his medications of choice after a meltdown, which probably had saved his marriage, together with other small steps towards full healing that always seemed just out of reach. His violent outbursts had gradually given way to numb resignation or silent withdrawal. Bits and pieces of his old self occasionally reappeared. Most of the severe Post-Traumatic Stress Disorder (PTSD) marriages from Vietnam didn't survive. His had, a rare and true miracle. Brenda stayed in bed, allowing Dane to decompress alone. He settled into the couch to await an expected phone call from Bret Horst to set up one of their frequent outings to the local rifle range.

Long-time friends, Bret and Dane had graduated from Gilbert High School together, and both were wed right after graduation. It was another miracle that Brenda had married an ordinary guy like Dane. While Dane was a little above average in sports and academics, except for his blond, surfer-dude looks and mischievous grin, he was not a standout in any way.

In their teens, Brenda had been the most strikingly-beautiful, vivacious girl imaginable, pursued by every male who laid eyes on her. She was still as beautiful, trim, and vibrant as she was back then.

Bret had been Gilbert High's Mr. Everything. Star quarterback, tall, athletic, handsome, and top student. Bret had doggedly pursued

Brenda. Although Bret could usually pick and choose any girl he wanted, he ended up marrying Kathy Burns. Kathy was a close second to Brenda in looks back then, and pretty adept at the spider and the fly game when she targeted a guy. They seemed happy and comfortable together.

On a steamy-hot August day after their high-school graduation in June, Dane and Bret were torn away from their new brides by the draft and thrown into the Vietnam war. After suffering through unending days of carnage and death as combat infantry soldiers, they were shipped home with profound irreversible wounds to their bodies and souls. Fifty-eight thousand of their brothers in arms never made it.

Dane and Brenda, and Bret and Kathy, reconnected after the war, bound inseparably together by their common trauma. As with most combat veterans, they soon realized that their families and friends couldn't comprehend or relate to the horrors they survived, nor to the hardened, withdrawn adults that returned home in place of the fun-loving, innocent kids they had known. Their once-wide social circles shrank to include only themselves and a few other veterans.

They settled back into the only town they had ever known. Bret bought the Gilbert Inn, the premier local watering hole. Dane found a comfortable management job with a large farm implement company. And just like that, twenty years flew by.

As the sun rose, Dane's living room began to get uncomfortably warm. He started fidgeting. It was never a good thing for Dane to have idle time alone with his thoughts. While he stared into space awaiting Bret's call, he begrudged the fact that he was so dependent on Bret to find any small measure of enjoyment in day-to-day life. The negative clouds began to build. It seemed like Bret had always carried a sort of smug superiority, just below the surface. Dane harbored some lingering jealousy of Bret's high school prowess. But Dane had Brenda, so he had won. Right? So Dane shouldn't be bothered by Bret's recent redirection of his attention from Kathy to Brenda, right? The thought that Brenda and Bret shared some private secret came out of nowhere and began tormenting him.

Dane's phone rang about 8:30. Disappointingly, Bret begged off their planned outing to the range. This had been happening a lot lately. Dane's mind -and imagination—plunged into a darkness that would quickly morph into a waking nightmare. Brenda seemed a little aloof lately. Were they seeing each other?

Dane grabbed his range bag and told Brenda he was heading to the range. Instead, he drove to a hidden spot behind their house, parked, and waited. An hour later his worst fears were confirmed. Bret's pickup truck slowly circled the block, parking half-way down. He watched Bret check his surroundings, and then slither into his back door like a guilty teenager.

Dane was paralyzed with rage. His "best friend" was trying to steal his only reason for living away from him. A half-hour later, the door opened. Bret sneaked back to his truck. Now fully in the grasp of his PTSD, Dane wondered, could he kill his best friend? For doing this, hell yeah! But it had to look like either an accident, or someone else's doing. Collateral damage. He needed a weapon untraceable to him, but traceable to someone else. He paused for a second. Was this any different than killing all those Viet Cong? Hey, it's just one more, right? Besides, what's left for me to live for if he steals Brenda? A potential ambush location materialized in his mind. He drove off to map it out.

A long ridge ran about 150 yards behind the rifle range parallel to the shooting bays. A thick stand of bushes and trees crowned the ridge. The ridge was accessible from its backside, hidden from the range. Dane concealed his truck, grabbed his spotting scope, and walked about 100 yards to the top of the ridge. He belly-crawled to the peak and aimed his scope through an opening in the brush down at the range, loving and hating what he saw: a clear line of sight to the shooting bay Bret always used, an exclusive part of the range away from the rest of it with metal targets reserved for highly qualified shooters. It was always busy. Ricochet control was strictly regulated, but always a danger. A tough shot for most, but Dane's instruction in sniper school during advanced infantry training and his long years of hunting experience put it within his reach. A well-placed angle of entry for a headshot might convince an investigator that a freak ricochet was to blame. What else could it be?

Dane headed into town, parked his truck, and wandered the streets in a fog, deciding what to do next. As he passed by the Gilbert Inn, Tony Vada, who had some vague service connection to the intelligence community, waved him in. The last thing Dane wanted was company, but to keep up appearances, he sat down. Tony simply said, "thanks, I need your help. I had a falling out with Bret. He threw me out the other day. Do you think he'd accept an apology?" Dane was taken aback by the mental jump-shift he now faced. "I, I guess so Tony. He can get pretty volatile about some things. I think it's always good to try to patch things up."

"Thanks," Tony said. "I pissed him off big time, but I've got to try." With that, Tony got up and walked towards the rear where Bret was bartending. His regular bartender hadn't shown up for work. Bret never noticed Dane. He didn't look like he was having a good day, and he darkened as Tony approached. Dane sat dumbfounded as after no more than a few words had passed between them, Bret burst from behind the bar and man-handled Tony out the door, throwing him onto the sidewalk. Stunned and thoroughly embarrassed, Tony loudly threatened to kill Bret. Bret ignored him and went back inside. Bewildered, Dane went out to console Tony after helping him up.

"I'm pretty rattled," Tony said. "Can you follow me home to be sure I make it?" Dane could hardly refuse.

Tony was extremely grateful. He wanted to repay Dane somehow. A drink of some expensive single-malt Scotch was offered, but Dane couldn't go there anymore, and politely declined. Tony thought a minute and then brightened. He offered Dane a rare invitation to see his extensive exotic gun collection. Tony rarely did this for anyone.

Tony led Dane to a heavy metal door at the rear of his house which he opened with a digital lock in Dane's plain sight with a simple four-number combination, 1-2-3-4, revealing a museum-worthy collection surely worth tens-of-thousands of dollars. Dane was stunned. He would have paid to see something like this.

Tony lovingly withdrew a magnificent vintage Winchester Model 70 with an expensive Leupold high-power scope, and custom bipod attached to the barrel, which Tony used only for hunting season. Dane was intrigued and got an education concerning the gun's capabilities and accuracy. It was always kept zeroed in, ready for immediate use with the match-grade rounds that sat below it. Tony carefully put the Seventy back in its place. The demons of fate had supplied Dane's missing parts for his plan. An easy rifle to steal. If the shot were traced to the ridge, Tony's threat would be recalled.

As Dane departed, Tony Caught him with a question and a concerned look. "You o.k.?" Dane mumbled he was fine and headed home, puzzled.

The next day, Bret called Dane in the late morning and sheepishly invited him to go to the range, apologizing for his missed outings. Dane politely declined. It was Dane's birthday, and Brenda was fixing him prime rib for a quiet birthday dinner alone. Dane hated parties. He had volunteered to do some errands and would have to pass.

It was too late to turn back. Dane left to run his errands. He drove by Tony's business. Spotting his truck there, he headed for Tony's house. With a pair of latex gloves, Dane carefully extracted the Seventy, several rounds of match-grade, and put them into a gun case he had brought. Closing the door, he left no traces of an intrusion. He headed directly to the top of the ridge and quickly dug a small trench to bury the Seventy in. He wiped the Seventy clear of any prints and set up in a prone position for his shot. Bret was at his bay on the busy range. Amazingly calm, Dane loaded, carefully set his sights on the side of Bret's head in a plausible spot for a ricochet, and slowly squeezed the trigger.

Nothing. His mind exploded in confusion and frustration. He reloaded and tried again. Click. He slid the bolt out of the gun, looking for the cause. The firing pin was missing. He had just attempted to murder someone with a stolen gun. In a panic, he threw the Seventy into its shallow grave, covered and concealed it well, and stumbled back to his truck.

As he pulled out on the main road, another truck approached from directly ahead and suddenly blocked him. Tony got out, a pair of binoculars hanging around his neck. Dane saw his life ending before his eyes. How could he have been stupid enough to think he could con someone with Tony's expertise in reading people and situations. Tony calmly said, "go get my Seventy. Then you better come with me." With no choice, he followed Tony to his house. To watch a videotape from a security camera of him stealing the rifle. A felony. Probably more, all told. Tony had him nailed.

"You were too interested in the Seventy. Especially the range it was zeroed in on. On top of that, you had a look on your face I know too well. You had in mind to kill someone. I knew you'd be back for it, so I disabled it. Funny that it was a sumbitch I'd just a' soon see dead." Tony laughed sardonically. "Maybe I should have let you do it."

Tony bored a hole in Dane with a thoughtful, piercing look in his eyes for several uncomfortable moments. Then, Tony pushed the "erase" button on the recorder, deleting the only evidence of the theft. "Go home," Tony said. "And find some other way to solve your situation."

Trembling, and without hope, Dane headed home. It was close to dinner time. He slowly opened the front door. Shouts of "Surprise!" and "Happy Birthday!" burst forth to greet him from a room filled with his closest friends, and Brenda, Bret, and Kathy. They formed a half-circle behind the Harley-Davidson Road King with pearl white paint and chrome everything except tires that he had lusted after for months. It had a huge bow on it. Of course. Bret was the only one close to Brenda big enough to have sneaked the thing into his house. Bret stepped up to hug him. "We love you, man. It's been a bitch keeping all this a secret from you!" Dane collapsed to his knees in tears. Nobody thought a thing about it.

Precious Cargo

Greg Picard

They'd chased the Jeep Waggoneer for almost 8 miles through the backcountry of the Cuyamaca Mountains. Wedged between the Cleveland National Forest and Anza Borrego Desert State Park gave the fugitive millions of places to hide if they lost him. Fortunately, the driver was dumb enough to eventually try to escape by turning off Highway 79 and onto the narrow road to Los Caballos Horse Camp -- a dead end for the car and almost for him. He'd smashed into a boulder in his haste to negotiate one of the turns. When Ranger Chris Becker pulled up behind the driver with gun drawn behind the cover of the park patrol Bronco, the driver stuck his hands out the window and begged, *"¡No disparen, me rindo!"* Which Chris, with his limited Spanish, figured it meant something like, "Don't kill me." His hands were still held high in the air outside the driver's side window as the ranger scanned the vehicle more closely.

"Great, another one that probably doesn't speak a word of English," Becker muttered to Eric Blake, who'd pulled in behind him and hustled up to crouch with Chris behind cover. "Several people in the car. Let's get 'em out where we can deal with them."

"I see heads peeking up from inside the Jeep...lots of them..way lots!" Eric marveled.

Yeah, and I'm pretty sure there's another one bent down in the front passenger seat," Chris said as he yelled to the driver, "Conductor, sal del auto con las manosen alto," and then followed it with "pone susmanosdetras de la cabesa! Rodilliase!" CHP had alerted all agencies to the vehicle, and that he thought they might be Mexican illegals when they had gotten away from one of their officers who stopped them for a speed violation, only to have them take off just as he got to their rear bumper.

The driver quickly dropped to his knees near the Jeep and laced his fingers behind his head.

"¡Todoslosdemásen el auto, salganuno a la vez!"

They were amazed as they then watched the eight more adults climb out one at a time and stand a few feet from the kneeling man. Some were obviously asking him questions, but Chris had little clue what was being said since his Spanish was mainly limited to arrest commands and medical injury questions. Beyond that, translating was a bumpy road. He looked at their worried faces and wondered what they all must be thinking.

"Check the vehicle in case there's maybe a midget left inside, and then cover me while I cuff the mule.

"You speak any English," Chris asked as he carefully felt for any weapons and then cuffed the driver.

"Yes, I speak English; I am an American citizen."

"Wow, wonders never cease. Eric, search the vehicle."

"You had them all stacked like cordwood on top of each other in that little Jeep! How could they even breathe? That can't have been fun."

"They are desperate. They will do anything to get into the U.S. to find a better life."

"I notice they are all women...fact is some look like they should be in Junior High. What kind of better life? Where were you taking them?"

The driver didn't respond, and Chris had him sit on the ground near the car while he walked over to Eric and pulled him aside.

"Your Spanish is better than mine. Find out what's going on with these females. This doesn't smell right. Start with the woman who was sitting up front with the driver. I think she may be part of this thing."

"You thinking abduction?"

"I don't know, just a hunch we've got something different going on," Chris whispered. "I'm gonna see if we can get Border Patrol over here quickly. And where is the CHP? They began this chase, where the hell did they go?"

Thirty minutes later, a Border Patrol SUV unit from the occasionally staffed checkpoint east of Julian pulled up behind them.

"Looks like you guys got a bonus load," he said as he walked over from his vehicle and inspected the group.

"Yeah, all packed in there smelling each other's armpits if not worse. My partner questioned one of them we think is working with the driver, and she isn't very forthcoming. I think this may be human trafficking," Chris said.

"Wouldn't be the first time. Economies get bad, and women are the worst hit. Seventy percent of the worlds' poor are women, and slavery is a great way to exploit the poor. They make up more than half the trafficked slaves."

"You're a veritable encyclopedia." Chris joked.

"It's serious stuff. Somewhere between twenty and thirty million people are modern-day slaves in this world. You'd be surprised how many are in the U.S. right under your nose cleaning houses, picking crops, or showing guys a 'good time' in bed or in some back alley. It's so perverted. Lots of them are just children. It's sick on so many levels."

Chris had been taught to look for trafficking in one of his ongoing law enforcement refreshers, but he had no idea how bad it really was, and that it could be happening right under his nose in his park.

"This is America...the land of the free," the Border Patrol Agent mocked. "We don't think about it much in our daily lives, but the slaves are everywhere. Funny, you'd think the black activist community and politicians would be all over it in sympathy, but all you hear is crickets. You can find slaves panhandling on the corner, doing landscaping or roofing, working in massage parlors, stripping in a club, or worse–like child prostitution rings. Phone chat lines are big for it, too."

"How can you tell it's slavery?"

"Well, if you see somebody accompanied, for instance to the doctor or Home Depot or the DMV, and one guy's always speaking for another person, be suspicious. It may not be just a language problem at all. They very well can be a 'handler' who goes along to keep the person from opening up or escaping. Plus, most of them are scared of deportation back to the hell hole they came from as much as they are unhappy about their slavery, so they often don't speak up...if they even know how to speak English."

An hour of babysitting later, a Border Patrol van arrived, and the group was loaded aboard with the driver and the front seat woman passenger taken in cuffs by the Border Patrol Officer in his SUV.

"What happens to them?" Chris asked.

"We'll put the driver and his helper in the county lockup. They're both citizens, and they'll likely let them bail out immediately without telling us when someone shows up with money. We'll likely never see the trial happen due to their mysterious disappearance, and the county will say 'thank you very much for the hefty bail money' as they wheelbarrow it down to their bank. The others will be held briefly in a federal detention center on charges of being undocumented in the country and told to return in several months for their hearing. Whereupon, they will disappear into the smoggy California night until we can catch them again...like that will ever happen!"

"You're kidding?"

"Wish I were," he said as he slammed the door and started the engine.

Chris watched as he pulled away, and the Triple "A" tow truck followed with the dangling Jeep. He wondered how a modern society like America could function long with this kind of approach to the law and being host to these kinds of perverts who abuse the vulnerable and the poor.

"Okay, back to being park rangers who spend all day smelling flowers and watching the deer and the squirrels like the public imagines," Chris said as he slapped Eric on the shoulder and smiled. "Which reminds me, have you finished that crime report on those three car burglaries from Yesterday?"

"On your desk, boss." Eric smiled.

As Chris got into his Bronco he heard one of his other rangers calling in to dispatch, "could I get some help in the Green Valley Campground, you won't believe the guy I've found down in the women's outhouse 'toilet pit' in a raincoat and pants with his camera. And tell them to bring the fire pumper, too. Maybe some bleach even."

Just another day, Chris thought to himself as he slammed the truck door and turned the key cranking over his white stallion.

"Hi, ho and away," he mumbled as he shook his head

Fatal Reflections

Sharon Sterling

Bruce glared at the ringing phone. He hated an interruption while he tweezed the hair in his ears. John always called at the wrong time, including this time. Bruce put the phone on speaker and continued grooming. He listened for a few seconds before he demanded, "You're just now sorting through all that junk? Your uncle inflicted that dilapidated old place on you six months ago. Why are you calling me now?"

John said, "I couldn't bring myself to do it so soon after he died. He left it to me in his will because he cared about me. You should come because you're my friend. Friends help each other."

Bruce held the hand mirror closer to his head and turned to see his reflection in the larger mirror. He reached in with the tweezers and jerked. Ouch! Too many hairs! His eyes watered, his nose ran. Swiping snot from his nostrils with the back of his hand, he flung down the tweezers, cursing. He turned and snarled into the phone, "What crap! I don't buy that fortune cookie twaddle. Friendship can go to hell."

"Bruce! Friendship is everything. It...." John's thought stopped him. Why argue? His relationship with Bruce had always been lopsided. It survived only because he tolerated Bruce's short-tempered ways. He asked, without much hope, "Then the answer is no?"

Bruce lifted his chin to look directly into the vanity mirror. His image blurred as unwanted memories of the many favors John had done for him began to surface. He turned toward the phone and yelled loud enough to bruise an eardrum, "Okay, but you owe me big time!"

An hour later, seated in his late-model convertible, ready to leave, Bruce took out his smartphone and tapped in the address John had given him. A map of the area lit the screen. He snorted. John had screwed up again. The house couldn't be located in that upscale business district. He reached for the door handle to go back inside, relieved at the prospect of escaping his promise. Well, better to check it out. When he reproached the stupid clod after making the trip for nothing, his anger would have more teeth.

After a short drive, he reached the business district to find that John's directions were right after all. Posh retail establishments had encroached on, but not totally obliterated, a neighborhood of large, two-story homes built in a more romantic and less commercial age. He turned the corner of a busy intersection and there it was the rundown old Victorian mansion. Damn! It meant he was in for an hour or so of physical labor, which he abhorred and usually succeeded in avoiding.

Grunting in disgust, he mounted the home's paint-bare stairs, walked across the creaking floorboards, and pushed open the heavy oak door. From the foyer, he could see John standing in what must have been the parlor, a room filled with what Bruce saw as an offensive mix of hoary antiques and hoarded trash.

His hostile gaze veered to a huge marble fireplace against the far wall. And held. For too long. Why; he didn't know. This fireplace, a pale stone monument to a bygone era, held the heart of the room. Around its mouth, smoke stains marred a once palliate sheen. Beneath its mantel, faint cracks spread down like the web of wrinkles on an old woman's face. Its hearth was a worn slick tongue, tinged with green. Near the hearth lay piles of moldering newspapers. To its left stood a cheap metal tray on rusted legs and to the right a tall wooden chair with a seat upholstered in tattered needlepoint. Bruce shuddered. A cold breath whooshed up his spine. He shook his head and looked away to break the spell. He walked into the room, pointed to the chair, and demanded "What kind of screwed-up decor is this?"

John smiled at him. "Eclectic antique. So many memories here, Bruce. This chair is a Victorian rose balloon-back fireside chair. Uncle sat in it every evening while he smoked his pipe."

"He was a demented old codger, wasn't he, gathering all this trash? Weak minds run in the family, do they?"

John didn't flinch at the insult. "There are good people in my bloodline, Bruce, but we do have some interesting leaves on one branch of the family tree. The story goes that my great-grandmother, the one whose husband built this house, was a strange sort. She had great powers of persuasion. She knew about herbs for healing people and animals and she had a small circle of devoted, older women friends around her. People whispered about her."

Bruce was barely listening. A shadowed outline above the fireplace drew him. "What was up there on the wall?"

"Just this old mirror." John moved to an object leaning across a corner of the room. It was a beautifully framed antique mirror. Gold leaf accented the wooden frame but the glass was now cloudy and scored with grey shadows from its deteriorating silver backing. John stroked the top of the frame with his fingertips. "It's not perfect but I love it. And look." He held up a greeting-card size piece of what looked like cardboard. He said, "I found this fastened to the paper that covers the back. It looks like cardboard but it's vellum, expensive stuff they used back then to write important things on. It says, 'Now new, e'er charmed, for mortal's sake, ne'er broken'. I can't figure out what it means."

"It means nothing. It's a stupid superstition and a stupid non-sequitur."

"A...a what?"

Bruce crossed his arms and tapped his foot on the threadbare Persian rug. "You've heard that breaking a mirror brings eight years of bad luck? And a non-sequitur is an illogical statement, an absurdity. Like: if a fire is out, it's no longer a fire; it's ashes. If a person is dead, he's no longer a person; he's a corpse. If a mirror were ever broken, it wouldn't be a mirror, it would be a pile of glass. Saying it's a mirror that's never been broken is stating the glaringly obvious. And if the stupid verse means it never will be broken, that's crap and nonsense."

For some reason, this patronizing lesson in semantics finally pierced John's bubble of good-will. His hands doubled into fists. He jammed them into his pockets and glared at Bruce. "I know you're smarter than me, Bruce, but I'm not enlightened by what you just said. And it was rude."

Bruce returned the insult, with interest. "Thanks for giving me a piece of your mind. I know you don't have much to spare. Here, I'll prove my point." He turned and grabbed a poker from the tool stand by the fireplace. He paused for effect, looking at John, then with an easy back-stroke, he tapped the mirror. It fell into three large pieces. "See? Now it's no longer a mirror."

John's mouth dropped open. He gaped from his friend to the floor and back again. He regained his breath and yelled, "Why did you do that? It was a family thing!"

"Spare me the drama, you sentimental idiot."

Tears threatened John's eyes as he looked into Bruce's face. "I thought you came here to help me, not ruin my inheritance."

Bruce wasn't listening. When the glass broke and fell, the mirror's wooden backing and frame stayed propped in the corner. Now it moved. Almost imperceptibly at first, then inch by inch, it tipped forward, prodded by nothing that could be seen. Bruce stared, unbelieving. The frame eased forward again. And again. When it reached its tipping point it crashed to the floor, impelled by—what? The mirror's frame and plywood back now lay over the broken glass. While they watched, the paper covering the plywood back slowly rolled down, as if pulled by an unseen hand.

Bruce shook off the hair-raising sensations in his body. He turned to stalk out, but something written in black calligraphy on the frame's back caught his attention. It was a verse of poetry, outlined by a large red pentagram. Alarm raced up his spine and spread over his head, a skullcap lined with nettles of fear. Horrified but captured, he read the inscription aloud:

Should foolish mortal fracture me,
Retribution follows if deliberate it be.
Tit-for-tat is wily witchcraft's key,
In just so many pieces, so shall he.

Darkness crept into the room, carrying the mustiness of age and the damp of decay. John's voice emerged in an anxious mumble, "I wonder what that means?"

Bruce flexed the muscles in his neck and shoulders, trying to shake off an inkling of the inscription's import. He glanced down at the poker still in his hand. He barely suppressed the urge to bludgeon John over the head with it. Instead, he sneered, "Your confidence in assuming I give a damn what it means is pathetic. This is ridiculous, all of it. I've had enough!" He threw down the poker and stalked out of the house. Heading toward his parked car, his hurried stride broke into a run. He reached the car, plunged into the soft leather seat, jammed the ignition button with his thumb, and screeched away from the curb, driven by dread, unaware of what he was fleeing.

At the same moment, a large paneled utility truck rounded the corner onto the two-lane road behind him. Bruce didn't see it in his rearview mirror, didn't see the name signed in red: *Window Magic by Sybil.* The truck suddenly accelerated. The driver jamming his foot on the brake. No use. He jerked the steering wheel sideways, from in the back of Bruce's car. No use. The truck swerved back, zeroed in on the little car, and increased its speed. Its driver was unaware the truck had found its prey.

Bruce saw the truck behind him. He swerved into the other lane. No use. The truck swerved again and closed in. Bruce stepped on the accelerator, pushed it to the floor. He felt its power then, exulted in the power as the car reached ninety-five miles an hour. Faster, it fishtailed, forcing other cars onto the shoulder of the road.

Bruce glanced into the rearview mirror. Sweat trickled into his eyes. The truck couldn't possibly go this fast but there it was, still on his bumper. Wetness spread over his fly and trickled down his crotch, wetting his ass. He looked up from the road, eyes sweeping back and forth, desperate for an escape route. He braked hard. Then harder still but the truck slowed in perfect synchrony.

The little sports car slowed almost to a stop. While it still rolled forward, Bruce leaped out, blind with fear. He stumbled, recovered, raced past the road's shoulder to a strip of grass and small trees. The truck turned. He glanced over his shoulder. It careened forward, jolted over the curb, onto the grass within feet of him. He dodged, ducked behind a tree. Too late.

Crash! The truck skidded sideways and smashed into the tree. The impact sent a plate glass window flying off the truck toward Bruce. He saw it move as if in slow motion. His mouth opened. Out poured a screech of terror and a string of saliva. The windowpane struck his face with a loud thwack, broke against his forehead. The top piece tilted forward, levering the razor-sharp bottom edge back. It sliced through his neck like a butcher knife through ham. His severed head dropped onto the dirt and rolled away while his body fell backward. At the same instant, the bottom piece of glass remained vertical as it fell, slicing the headless body's midsection clean through. Ropes of steaming viscera and bits of other organs oozed out, carried on gouts of blood. Contents of bladder and bowel poured forth.

Crash! Screech! Those noises gave way to pops, sputters, and groans, while blood flowed and life waned. The last sounds that Bruce's hair-trimmed ears registered were gurgles of disbelief, horrified mewlings, and these words whispering in his dying brain:

Like the mirror that had never been broken
Is now three shards of glass,
Bruce, in three shards, not a person,
Is now a corpse on the grass.

Good Karma

Roger Antony

As far as I know, the only prospectors on Banning Creek are Harvey Webster and me.

Harvey has lived his entire life in Yavapai County. When his wife died he sold his 280 acres and moved to Terra Verde, a town of about 25,000 located at the intersection of Arizona Routes 69 & 89.

He'd been a rancher and worked daily from sunup to sundown. After moving into a house off Senator Highway, he wanted something to keep him busy. He turned to prospecting.

Harvey would leave his house in the morning after having breakfast, packing a snack and filling a thermos with coffee, and walk to Banning Creek where he'd spend his mornings 7 days a week prospecting. He usually returned home by 1 o'clock and by 2 was in bed having a nap.

I'd met Harvey 2 years ago after moving into a subdivision near Banning Creek. One day soon after we moved in, I was walking through the National Forest along Trail 81 when I observed a man with a portable sluice box along the creek. Intrigued, I went off trail and spent several hours talking with him.

He was reticent to talk about his finds, but was a wealth of knowledge about prospecting for placer deposits. He's the one that got me interested in the hobby.

He explained that he uses his sluice box when the creek is running to capture gold flakes and when it's dry he walks the creek bed with a shovel looking for gold nuggets.

Last summer, I found several pea-size nuggets buried beneath tree roots in the dry creek bed.

They were nothing like the 2 oz. gold nugget Harvey pulled out of the creek bed. After finding it, he invited me to see his entire gold nugget collection.

When I asked what stretch of the creek he'd been in when he found the nugget, he clammed up. All he would say was, "South of the city."

I'd already figured out that much. I also knew that if I'd put Harvey's hand over a candle flame or twisted his arm behind his back, he wouldn't reveal where he'd found his prize nugget.

Last week, I walked a section of the creek north of where Trail 330 crosses the dry creek. As usual, I found nothing, so this week I decided to prospect south of the trail crossing. It was slow going as I turned over rock after rock and dug with my small hand spade.

It was hot so after 2 hours I took a break and sat on a large granite rock in the middle of the dry creek bed and ate a package of peanut butter crackers, an apple, and drank cold coffee from my thermos. When I was done, I found a tree that concealed me from both the path and the creek and relieved myself.

When I stepped back into the creek bed I saw a glint from a stone partially hidden beneath an exposed root of an old Emory oak. The glint came from a rock which at first looked to be the size of a large marble.

It took quite a bit of effort to remove the gold nugget, but when freed it was the length of a hot dog and shaped like a banana. I guessed it weighed 6 to 7 oz.

I turned the gold nugget over and over. Each time my heart skipped a beat as I realized I'd found a substantial nugget with gold interlaced with rose quartz making it look like the stripes on a barber pole.

After finding the gold nugget I called it a day, left the creek bed, and walked home along the trail. When I arrived home I found my wife, Lydia, in the kitchen making soup. When she saw me she asked, "Find anything?"

My usual answer was, "No," so she didn't expect me to pull a gold nugget from my pocket and put it on the countertop next to her cutting board.

"Oh, my god," she said.

I turned it over so she could see the entire exterior surface.

Pointing with the knife in her hand she asked, "How much gold?"

"I'm guessing 2 oz. or so. When do we eat?"

"Dinner at 6," said Lydia.

I walked out of the kitchen detoured to the bathroom then went to my studio and cleared a section on my lowest shelf where I keep my wallet and keys and made room for the gold nugget. I stood back and admired my find.

At dinner, Lydia talked about her plans to have 11 women over on Friday to play Bunco, what she planned to fix, and my role in cleaning, setting up the card tables, and getting chairs down from the attic.

We didn't discuss my find, but while we were gathering our plates and taking them to the kitchen after dinner I said, "Maybe I should sell it."

"Good idea," she said.

"I could use the money to buy a trailer."

"Are you talking about a travel trailer or one to carry trash to the dump?"

I said, "Travel trailer."

"Aren't they expensive?"

"I'm thinking about an older model."

"Herb," Lydia said putting her hands on her hips. "What are we going to do with a travel trailer?"

"Go traveling," I said. Seeing the look on her face like I was a delinquent child, I said, "It's just a thought."

"Herb, when was the last time we went on a vacation and spent time at a KOA campground?" It was a rhetorical question which she quickly answered. "Never, and I'm not starting now."

"Well, maybe we could use the money for a new car."

"Our cars are fine. How about giving the money to the food bank?"

I didn't quite hear her so I said, "I guess I can put it in the bank," and walked away.

Lydia raised her voice. "Herb, I said food bank."

I returned to the kitchen. "You want me to sell the gold nugget and give the money to the food bank?"

"Why not, you'll find another nugget, besides its good karma."

I repeated her words aloud, "Good Karma."

Lydia said, "They could use the money."

"So could we, with inflation and everything," I said.

Lydia raised her voice, "Herb."

"You want me to give them the nugget?"

"Herb, write them a check."

I studied Lydia's face wondering if she was going to smile and say, 'I was only teasing. Buy yourself some new clothes, let's go out to dinner, let's splurge on something,' but she didn't. She just stared at me until I said, "You want me to sell my nugget and write them a check?"

"Isn't that what I just said?"

A week later I sold the nugget and received a check for $1,800. It was less than I had anticipated, but when the buyer provided me with a plausible reason why his price was fair, I agreed.

I asked the gold buyer to make the check out to the Terra Verde Food Bank. He questioned me, but I insisted.

On Monday morning, I drove to the food bank where I found an older woman sitting behind an old gray metal desk. Her name tag indicated she was Shirley B. Behind her in the warehouse I could see 3 women stocking food on shelves.

I pulled out the $1,800 check.

She looked at the amount and thanked me. She didn't seem phased by the amount of the check, which I took to mean that it was not unusual to receive large contributions.

When she took the check, I kept hold of it longer than I needed to. The situation reminded me of the scene from the movie *Ghost* where Oda Mae Brown played by Whoopi Goldberg hands a $4 million check to a nun while Sam Wheat, played by actor Patrick Swayze, assures Oda Mae Brown it's the right thing to do.

Shirley smiled when I released the check. I returned the smile. It was done.

She opened a drawer and lifted the lid on a metal box and placed the check inside then withdrew a receipt pad.

"Can I get your name and address?" Shirley asked.

Even though the check had the name, address and phone number of Assay Gold Partners printed on it, she wanted my information.

I said, "I don't need a tax receipt."

"You never know. What's your name?"

We talked for a few minutes. Before I left, she thanked me again.

I felt good as I walked out of the food bank.

The food bank had become very busy since the coronavirus infections had hit Terra Verde. People in town and around the county were losing their jobs and were unable to pay their mortgage, insurance, car payments, utilities, and buy food for their families.

Lydia had been right; others needed it more than we did. When I returned to the house she asked me how it went.

I explained to her my emotions prior, during, and after handing over the check.

Lydia said, "Good. Your nugget will do some good in the community."

I was standing in the kitchen waiting for our Mr. Coffee to finish brewing when Lydia asked me what Harvey had done with the gold nuggets he'd found.

"He has them displayed on a shelf."

"What good does that do?" When I didn't reply she added, "Does Harvey need the money?"

"I doubt it," I said.

"Why doesn't he sell them and give the money to the food bank?"

"I don't know. You'll have to ask him," I said.

"Next time you see Harvey, tell him what you did with your nugget."

"You think he'll sell his nuggets and give the money to the food bank just because I did? You don't know Harvey."

"Tell him anyway. I plan on telling Betsy," said Lydia.

I'm not sure Betsy was his girlfriend or should I say woman friend, but they were close and whenever I saw Harvey in town I saw her with him. She's maybe a year or two younger than Harvey, but both looked to be in their mid-seventies.

I asked, "Do you really think me telling him what I did will cause him to do the same?"

"Maybe, maybe not, but if you tell him that you're going to keep looking for nuggets and you're going to give the food bank all the nuggets you find, it'll make a difference."

"When did I say I was going to give away everything I find?"

"You didn't, but you will," said Lydia.

"Why?" I asked.

"It's the right thing to do. It'll make you feel good when you're out prospecting and again when you give the food bank a check."

I didn't say anything to Lydia, just poured my coffee and returned to the back patio to read a book.

I couldn't admit to Lydia then that the idea of searching for gold and giving it away felt uplifting.

The next morning I saw Harvey with his prospecting gear step off the trail and head for the creek bed. He heard me and stopped. In a brief conversation, I told him what I'd done with my nugget.

He scoffed at me. "Are you insane?"

"It was Lydia's idea, but it makes sense," I said.

"What makes sense?" asked Harvey.

I said, "It's no different than catch and release when fishing. It's the challenge and thrill of catching a fish. It's the same with prospecting. You could throw the gold nugget or flakes back into the creek, but it makes much more sense to release it into the community and help the families that are struggling."

Harvey stared at me then stalked off down the dry creek bed shaking his head.

A week later I found a small gold nugget and like before, sold it and had the check made out to the Terra Verde Food Bank. Shirley B. at the food bank said when I handed her the second check, "We really appreciate your help in filling our shelves."

I nodded and looked past Shirley into the warehouse and saw a dozen women, some with little children, picking food off the shelves and putting it into their shopping carts.

Two weeks later I saw Harvey. He had a smile on his face and seemed cheery, not an emotion I associated with Harvey.

When we were closer he said to me, "Herb, how are you doing?"

It was more cordial than in the past. "I'm fine and you?"

"I sold several nuggets to Gold Assay Partners."

I nodded.

"I had them make out a check to the food bank."

I smiled."Did Lydia talk to Betsy?"

"Sure did. Your wife's right and so is Betsy. Doing good for others is good for you," Harvey said.

Harvey and I started working as a team and before the monsoon started and the dry creek became a flowing stream, we found 2 small nuggets which we sold and proudly gave the proceeds to the food bank. The last time we visited the food bank, we went together and handed the clerk a check.

I felt good. Harvey, not one to smile, had a broad grin on his weathered face when Shirley B. thanked us for supporting Terra Verde's Food Bank. Before we left, she shifted into her Southern drawl and said, "Y'all come back real soon. We appreciate your business."

The Hanging Gardens

Sharon Boerbon Hanson

"There's only one piece of your chocolate torte left," Maurey said, sliding her eyes sideways at Louise and lifting one eyebrow. "And I should have it. After all, you need to be especially nice to me, as I'll probably go to prison when you die."

They both laugh at her statement. Their private joke. Her reference comes not because she'll have killed Louise. No. And it won't be because she indulged in some provocation that assaults conventional mores or sensibilities.

Well. Ok. I'm lying about that bit.

Maurey will have.

Maurey promised to lodge Louise's dead and naked body in a tree for vultures to eat. So, she *will* be committing an illegal act—unless it becomes permissible to drape a dead body from a birch branch.

She pledged herself to that undertaking as Louise finds all current disposal practices unnatural. Indeed, most procedures in vogue void the natural cycle of life from death.

As Hamlet said, "*A man may fish with the worm that hath eat of a king, and eat of the fish that hath fed of that worm.*"

That's all Louise wants, an **organic** option. She's eaten birds and animals all her life. Her mantra says it all. When she dies, let them eat her.

That desire removes cremation for her cadaver. The thought of burning into a greasy heap of dirty black cinders makes her flesh creep.

Quivers of disgust shimmied down and up her spine when she heard about the potential to rid the world of the dead by dissolving them in lye and flushing them down the drain. Talk about putting the "grim" in Grim Reaper. The thought of using alkaline hydrolysis, an industrial solution, on a *human body* offends her. Deeply.

So does burial in a parking plot. Stuck in one place for eternity—yuck!

Louise loves to travel. She'd prefer her family take her corpse on a last vacation—maybe to Alaska or Hawaii. Stuff her into an extra-strength Hefty bag with some dry ice, toss it into a car or steamer trunk, and away they'd go. After hoisting Louise into the embrace of a towering pine or palm tree they'd enjoy snow and skiing or sun and surf. Her second mantra: let's put some *f-u-n fun* into "funeral."

Yes, give her any natural choice. If not a tree, maybe the sea. Groceries for the birds or food for the fishes; either would be fine.

The sea seems a particularly sanitary solution. Hordes of humans drown in the sea, but have you ever read about it in a pollution report? No. Because the bodies rot away or are consumed. Life from death. The continuation of the natural cycle.

Consider the advantages to disposal at sea, such as hiring Hearse Boats and their crews to ferry the dead and family to a plunge point. Such a scheme could revive a part of the flagging American economy by offering a whole new line of work for down-sized Caribbean cruise line personnel. Think of the possibilities! Get a tan, dance under romantic starry skies, plop granny in the sea–whole families relishing their time together while saying good-bye.

If they jettison corpses one per mile, dropped like pearls off a string, the vast oceans would never fill up. Even a plethora of dead from plagues or major catastrophes could easily be accommodated. Consider the ripple effect: with the injection of an increased protein diet, our vanishing sea life would prosper to reproduce more fish to feed hungry living humans.

Still, Louise prefers a spruce tree to the sea. Although, if this method catches on, logistics problems may crop up. What if large numbers of dead drip like icicles on oaks along neighborhood streets?

First, it'd be ghoulish to see bodies suspended from tree limbs by rigor-mortised elbows–especially on maple-lined boulevards close to home. And second, birds and beasts removing flesh from the dead could be problematic. Vultures, ravens, crows, and scavenging beasts scare school children.

Tasteful biers– open-top tree houses for the departed–need to be designed. Simple, plain platforms, so not to impede birds and animals, would be inexpensive. As a convenience for families that suffer vertigo, artful arrangements of low rock slabs could hold the remains of their loved ones.

The creation of special "suspension" zones could spur our economically-hit building industry. We'd place the zones downwind of population centers, of course. Death doth reek.

Owing to hygienic concerns (such as bird droppings) and safety issues (such as the unfettered roaming about of flesh-rending animals) we'd need to preserve areas outside city limits for what Louise envisions as "The Hanging Gardens."

Large gardens to service entire states, or small branches placed in every county. Think of the revitalization of an economically depressed area, if it became a "destination."

All the usual accouterments of tourist travel would be needed. Hotels and restaurants with attendant staff. And service jobs specific to death would swell employment: all-weather singers and hoisters, scat-shovelers, and gas-mask vendors are only a few of the new occupations; surely many other support roles would develop.

It's not like Louise's idea is unusual. Tree "burial" has antecedents in other cultures. In Tibet, after lighting a small juniper fire, a tomden, or butcher, places a body on a rock platform. He slices it from head to toe exposing the flesh and bones. Then, vultures descend and feast. After the birds pick the bones clean, the tomden pulverizes them and mixes them with the brain and flour. A pastiche made for hawks and ravens and nothing remaining after dessert but wisps of juniper smoke.

Okay, it may take a while for that to catch on.

In reality, most post-life rituals developed for the comfort of mourners. And naturally, Louise wants her loved ones comforted. Certainly, she knows her disposal request will *dis*comfort them.

But rather than erecting a tomb in some boneyard, She requests her family plant a rose bush, her favorite flower, in their garden. A tea rose, with its connotation of remembrance, and next to it, a small marker engraved with her name. How delightful. Their garden could grow ever more profuse with a plant signifying every important departure. Eventually, they could edge a garden walk with tiny tombstones, each bearing a loved one's name.

Consolation really is about expectations, however; so Louise has begun a comfort campaign to help her family adjust to the idea of a dangling deceased.

And there is another person's comfort to consider. All this focus on being swag in a swamp oak keeps Louise's thoughts on the *aftermath* of the event she dreads. So, she puts a bit of levity in a deadly serious consideration.

There is one other possible disposal for her—although it would cheat Maurey of her chosen chore as hangwoman—medical research. She'd offer her body to science. But only if they'd promise, after using it, to place her leftover bits and pieces on a bird feeder.

On Thin Ice

Tom Spirito

We were an odd threesome, Glen, Benny, and I. Glen was tall, Nordic, and had a ripped torso. Benny had jet black hair, was darker skinned, shorter than Glen and me, and extremely wiry, almost skinny. He also had a large, shapeless red birthmark on his forehead which I don't think we ever took much notice of. My body shape had exiled me to shopping in the young boys' clothing store section embarrassingly referred to as the "husky" department. A definite result of my Italian heritage and dietary choices. We had met in grammar school and were good friends through junior and senior high school. Because of his slight build, we nicknamed Benny "Topo." That name came from a cute and funny mouse puppet character on the Ed Sullivan Show by the name of Topo Gigio. Eventually, we tired of that and would at times call him Biag', short for Biago which was his given name. I was touched by the tender name Benny's Mom and Grandmother called him, which was "Hijo." They said it with so much love, much like my Dad when he called me son. I, on the other hand, was stuck for a while with the nickname "Thelma," thanks to a substitute teacher in the sixth grade who tried to read attendance without her glasses. It took a couple of years for the laughter to die down on that one. We were all in the same grade, but Glen had been left-back and was a year older. Benny and I looked up to Glen. He was no dummy and would be voted the "Most Witty" in our high schools' graduating senior class of five hundred students.

The three of us enjoyed sharing our comic books, toys, and board gaming for hours on end. One of our more exciting activities were our BB gunfights. We would put on our full-length yellow raincoats, swim goggles, and our fathers World War Two helmets and run around in the woods shooting at each other. If you heard a "ping," you knew you hit someone in the helmet. If you heard a "whap," you knew you hit your target on his raincoat. If you heard a howl of pain, you knew you got a piece of bare skin. Benny and Glenn were both expert marksmen with firearms which resulted in my always going home with a few mini red badges of courage on my exposed parts. We were always shooting or throwing something at some target or other. Many a plastic model boat was torn asunder as it floated to its doom down a nearby creek through a gauntlet fusillade of BB's and firecrackers. Besides being a crack shot, Benny's "superpower" was being the best at throwing anything that I had ever witnessed. He could launch a rock, a baseball, or a dirt bomb with deadly precision and at longer distances than I ever imagined possible. I don't know why he ever bothered with a gun. Glen had a great sense of humor and could impersonate many Hollywood personalities. He did an exceptional John Wayne, funny walk, and all. He could always make us laugh. Our backgrounds were also a bit dissimilar. Glen was of German descent. Benny was half Italian and half Pilipino, the result of an American G.I. and his war bride. I was a third-generation Italian, 100% Napolitano. Glenn and I had one thing in common, both our Mom's had passed away. We often ate at Benny's home where his Mom and Grandmother fed and doted on us.

I was fourteen and it was a cold day. The three of us had an adventure planned and there was no way the weather was going to stop us. We had our hunting licenses, ammo, and shotguns. Glenn knew a place called the pine barrens out in Suffolk County, Long Island. It was public land near the county landfill. Benny had arranged for his Mom to drop us off out there in the morning and pick us up in the afternoon. The day was to be an exciting rat hunt. Supposedly the barrens were crawling with these vermin, and it was perfectly legal to shoot them. We even thought we would be performing a public service. After all, didn't these rodents cause the Black Plague? If the gunplay described in this story seems a bit cavalier remember this was the early 1960's. Besides, Benny and Glen were both competitive shooters on our school's riflery team and very serious about gun safety. They took me under their wing and were on my case if I exhibited any poor weapon handling traits. The prime rule was that a safe gun is one that is pointed in a safe direction at all times. I always thought the safest gun was an unloaded gun.

Wrong, my buddies instructed me because you should never assume a gun is unloaded. You must treat all guns, all the time as if they were loaded and therefore dangerous. Amen.

Ben's Mom dropped us off and we wandered around the pine barrens, but I don't remember seeing even one creepy, crawly rat the entire day. There were, what we assumed were rat dens in the side of a few dirt embankments, so we shot a couple of rounds into the holes to see if that would start a little action. Nothing happened, so we stopped and had a snack. It was looking as if this wasn't going to be much of an adventure. Heck, we barely got to shoot our guns. We were meandering in a large arc through the barrens figuring we'd come back out about where we entered. We were a bit off course and came to a body of frozen water. It seemed to originate from a large corrugated metal pipe. The small pond was frozen from one end to the other and covered an area which discouraged us from walking around and making a prudent detour. Believing the December chill was sufficiently cold to ensure the ice was thick enough we decided to take the shortcut across it. Benny, being the lightweight of our party, put his foot on the ice to test our theory out. He seemed satisfied that it would hold him so he headed across. After crossing the approximately thirty-foot waterway safely, he turned to Glenn and me, smiled, and waved us on. Glenn went next. He was our middleweight contender. No problem, not a hint of a crack. Having been raised on second helpings of pasta since I had teeth, I was definitely the heaviest of our trio. About halfway across an audible crackling of the ice brought me to a halt. Benny and Glens' heads popped up, smiles gone now, eyes widening. I was stiff as a mannequin, afraid to move. "Don't worry," Glen said. It's not very deep, "Come on!" The next sound wasn't more encouragement from the far shore, but a loud crunching underfoot as the ice gave way and I settled to the bottom.

Glenn was right, it wasn't very deep. I only went in as far as my crotch. But what we hadn't foreseen was that this wasn't just a drainage of frozen water. As our noses began to inform us, this was raw sewerage. I was still standing at attention, my shotgun held across my chest. I was frowning like never before, my lips began to quiver. This was no time to cry I told myself. I willed my feet to move up and down through successive steps, breaking through the ice and sloshing through the muck until I was standing next to my two best buddies. My two best buddies were backing away and wanted nothing to do with me. Could you blame them, I stunk to high heaven. I must have looked so sad and uncomfortable that they took pity on me. They ventured just close enough to take my gun and hand me a stick to wipe off a portion of the clinging slurry. Once they were comfortable with my situation the merciless laughter began.

Luckily we were only a short distance from our pick up location where our ride was waiting for us. Benny's Mom took one look and a whiff of me and was momentarily speechless. I made a move toward the car and she loudly commanded, "Oh no you don't!" "Take off those pants," I was shocked and humiliated. I was soaked in crap to my nuts and smelled worse than a compost heap on a dairy farm in August, and now I would have to disrobe in front of my friends' Mother. My situation was so irretrievably, irreversibly inescapable that I felt time itself had stopped. Benny's Mom held her nose and retrieved a filthy old blanket from under the spare tire in the car trunk. I dropped my dungarees along with my dignity and wrapped myself in the blanket. I was seated in the center of the back seat of her 1960 something Rambler, trying not to touch anything or anyone. Everyone else was in the front seat trying not to touch, look at, or smell me. The car windows were closed only for a moment as everyone's eyes began to water, and Benny's Mom cried out, "Open the windows!" It was now freezing outside and inside of the car as we turned onto Sunrise Highway and picked up speed. We had a thirty-minute ride back home and the windows would remain wide open for the entire trip, and for several days after. In our wake cars seemed to move away from us, and when we stopped for red lights I could see heads turn, eyes squint, lips frown, and fingers pinching noses. It was a bit warmer when we stopped for the red lights, but without the breeze the smell was intense! I was beyond mortified, and this would be the longest thirty minutes of my life up to that time. I have to qualify that statement because I was only fourteen and there would be many more mortifying occasions to come over the next sixty years.

We lost touch with Glenn shortly after high school, but Benny and I stayed close friends for fifty years. Usually, these kinds of experiences have a way of becoming humorous in the retelling as the years go by. Thankfully, Benny nor any of the other participants ever spoke of this again in my presence. I was certainly blessed with good, kind friends. But let's face it, this story just ***STINKS!***

Picture Perfect Family

Sharon Boerbon Hanson

It's Christmas, and by some happy confluence, all of June's brothers and sisters are in St. Paul. As befitting the de facto matriarch of the family, they have gathered in her home.

Wealthy, moved-away-to-Portland Ted and wife Tina. Looking for a handout or a scamming opportunity, youngest brother, Jimmy. Here with six of his eight children Roland, his wife now run away, no one knows where or with whom. Lives-in-town Carmen and husband Joe, the sophisticated pair. And Sadie, mother to the brood.

June loves family. June loves Sara. Sara's family. Ever since she married June's youngest son four months ago, as June confided. June's elder son, her favored, is here too, no spouse yet.

June brightens, raisin eyes twinkling. She straightens in her chair. "A family photo!" We have to have a family picture." She hauls herself from her armchair, her throne, to the breakfront along one dining room wall to retrieve her camera. In its mirrored backsplash the image of her dark curly hair, close-cropped, haloing her round smiling face, bops up and down as she looks in cupboards and drawers.

"All the family by the sofa!" She commands; camera firmly in hand. She also has family firmly in hand, for although she is the middle child and youngest daughter, despite the fact her mother is in residence in St. Paul, June, laughter, and gossip always ready, is both the family center and leader.

Uncles and aunts, nieces, and nephews rise and cluster. June thrusts the camera into Tina's hands. Sara, smiling broadly, proudly, joins the milling group.

June squints at Sata. "Oh, just the family, it's a *family* picture, dear."

"She is family," Sadie snarls at her youngest child.

"Oh, of course, Mom, of course, I only meant, just the *real* family."

Arms tight against her body Sara moves stiffly, eyes wide and dry, to Tina's side. Tina, wife of Ted, is waving her hands guiding people this way and that, composing the most pleasing arrangement. "June," she calls, "settle everyone in the best arrangement."

As June bustles with command, Tina turns to Sara. She holds her auburn head high, looking out toward the family. She is eight inches taller than Sara, but her soft voice floats down only to the shorter woman, "I've been married to her brother for twenty-five years. You won't see me in any "family" photo. You will notice Carmen's husband in them. Perhaps it's just that June defines family by gender.

Her words don't console Sara, for she realizes June doesn't define family by heart.

*

At sixteen Sara met the woman who epitomized caring motherhood in her unworldly mind. June would raise not a hand nor a belt nor a tree branch to the back and legs of her children. Never had she slapped a face nor punched an eye. June watched closely, lovingly after her sons.

When Ray, her firstborn, entered the workhouse, where drunken drivers go after being picked up too many times, June castigated the system that let him down, the cops with no compassion, the friends who let him drive drunk.

When his car engine burned out owing to lack of oil, she railed at his friends for not telling Ray what the red dashboard light meant.

When he indulged in a flirtation with the young mother next door, "the devious harlot" received alternating shunning and derision for leading June's son astray.

Knowing Ray's culpability in all the escapades, Sara longed for a mother who would instantly and unreservedly take her side against the world.

The desire to cloak herself in unreserved, undeserved approval may have been as strong a draw to marriage as June's son himself. June called Sara, daughter. She welcomed her with the words, "you are now the daughter I've always wanted." How Sara loved those words. How Sara loved her.

The first time Greg had an extramarital affair, June wondered how Sara failed him. Was Sara too demanding when he worked so hard? Perhaps Sara didn't keep the baby quiet and drove a frustrated Greg from the house? Perhaps Sara didn't try hard enough to provide what her son needed.

Too young, too needy for love, Sara hadn't understood that the license granted June's family would continue, no matter the transgressions; and as an outsider, no sin against her counted.

*

The day after it happened, Sara's children relayed the news that her former mother-in-law had died. She had not been called when June lay dying—many years had passed; Sara was the past. But Sara already knew.

The day June died, Sara, lively in her living room, exercised to the pulse of Abba. After one strenuous routine, she rested, listening to the music. As Sara stood, heart-thumping, a swirl of energy zipped around her head. It wove down and around her, as if winding Sara up with an invisible thread. Gnat-like, it thrust at her face, her shoulder, forced her attention to it. Abba faded into the background; Sara concentrated on the frenetic energy insistently dive-bombing her. And she knew.

"It's all right, June," she said, audibly. "I know you loved me as best you could. I loved you, too. The past is past. It's all right now. You can go."

June's energy unwound, fizzed into the unknown leaving the known behind.

The Hunted

S Resler Nelson

"How did I get into *this* mess?" I said aloud, as I climbed out of my 4x4 open Jeep and slammed the door. My Jeep had died in the middle of nowhere. I guessed something could've gone wrong with the ignition switch, but I didn't know auto mechanics well enough to fix it. How absurd! Here I was, Jack Reed, a big-game hunter who'd brought down any number of wild animals in Africa, and now *I* was the potential prey?

I'd broken down in a stand of acacia and gum trees. Yeah, I had my high-powered rifle and ammo, but so what? If elephants came through the forest and I riled them, they might charge regardless of the risks. Poaching and trophy hunting had forced wildlife into survival mode. Elephants could flip the Jeep and make short order of me. I'd witnessed their ire firsthand.

Often mature elephants formed a circle and kept their youngsters in the middle to protect them. Then they'd stand their ground, or retreat into the woods if they could do so safely. I hoped there were no elephants nearby. I'd neither seen nor heard them, but they could stroll through the woods with amazing stealth. They walked so softly you'd only hear the snapping of branches.

And what about the other big five? Cape buffalo, rhinos, lions, and leopards had been hunted and harassed until *they* felt vulnerable, too. Thanks to hunters like himself, even photo safari-goers were sometimes treated as enemies, especially in this part of Zimbabwe.

I was far enough from water to discount rhino, but not buffalo and the big cats. On the edge of the savannah, I could see the wide grasslands through the trees, but anyone flying over wouldn't see my Jeep. If I couldn't flag down some wayward hunters, I'd be stuck here for hours, even days.

"Serves me right," I muttered and kicked a tire. I was losing it and getting angry wasn't going to solve my dilemma. I had to have a plan. I pulled out my cell phone but didn't find a signal. Not surprising.

Service was spotty in this area. Technically, I was supposed to be with a professional hunter, but I'd shrugged that restriction aside today.

My first mistake...my older brother, Ralph, and I had gone separate ways this morning. Ralph was the quintessential hunter, a certified professional, sometimes leading me, and often guiding other hunters. Lately, however, I'd found myself holding back, losing interest in the "sport." I'd come to the conclusion that sitting behind a blind after we'd set out bait to lure in a big cat was not hunting. Neither was hiding near a watering hole to surprise a thirsty trophy animal. It was stalking, and I'd grown weary of it.

Ralph and I were becoming opposites. We'd never looked alike except for our brown eyes. I was younger, leaner, and clean-shaven. We usually hunted together as backup for each other, and so I'd be "legal." But we'd gotten in a fight last evening. Not a fistfight, though we'd almost come to blows over a lion. Here's how it had happened.

We came across the lion at a watering hole about dusk. The aged lion was outstanding–a full black mane, regal head, commanding presence. And he led a small pride of two lionesses with cubs.

"Shoot him," Ralph whispered, as we hid downwind. "He's bigger than any lion I've brought down, and you haven't even shot one."

Frankly, I didn't want to–not this one. The pride drank peacefully at the small pond. A setting sun backlit them in soft, gilded hues and spread golds and reds over the shimmering water. How could I end such beauty?

"No," I answered in a soft murmur.

"You're such a wuss. If you don't do it, I will." At that moment, I'd had it with Ralph. He'd kill the lion, but I could aim to miss, and at least the magnificent lion would have a chance. To my brother's credit, I knew he wasn't after the lionesses.

I shot, and my heart sank. I hit him, and he went down. The pride scattered, and as suddenly as the old lion fell, he rolled upright and dragged a hind leg, as he lurched into the tall grass. Ralph said, "Let's go after him!" I resisted, and that's when we almost fought...until I backed down. After all, he was my brother.

Disgusted, Ralph headed back to the Jeep with me in tow. It was dark now, and even he'd given up for the night. I slept fitfully through the hours, thinking about the lion in pain and peril. I felt like a jerk for leaving him to suffer, maybe bleed out and die. But if we'd gone after him, Ralph would have finished him off and kept him as a trophy. I hoped he would survive.

So, here I was the next morning, fourteen hours later, looking for the lion I'd shot, figuring he was in the area near where we'd hunted last evening. I'd driven into the trees thinking the lion would be looking for shade. I assumed my brother was out searching, too, and the lion's fate depended on who found him first.

I gathered my Winchester Magnum with my ammo belt, binoculars, cell phone, water, and headed into the open. A "road" skirted the small forest revealing hoof, paw, and even elephant prints, as well as a few tire tracks. Just off the road, I saw a lion hunkered down about a hundred feet away. I glanced back and could still see my Jeep.

How long had he been there? As I peered closely, I realized he was the lion I'd shot. His right hind leg was caked with blood, and he seemed distressed. He crouched like the Sphinx so he'd *appear* ready to attack, but I doubted he could even stand. If I didn't intervene, he'd die. A predator would finish him off, if not a hunter.

I backed away and sprinted to the Jeep, glancing over my shoulder to make sure he wasn't after me. But the lion didn't move. In the back of my vehicle, I found a pail and filled it half full of water. He had to be thirsty, and I shouldn't offer food. Water was his immediate need.

Then I made a tough decision. I left my rifle and took a pistol I hadn't used for several days. I figured if he smelled gunpowder from the rifle I'd used yesterday, he'd be more guarded. Many animals have an amazing sense of smell, much greater than we humans.

I found a sturdy stick and carried it as a staff. I approached within ten feet of the lion and placed the pail of water on the end of the stick. Each move was slow and measured, non-threatening. Then I inched the pail toward him. He lifted his head as if smelling the water.

Slowly, I let the stick reach out and placed the pail in front of him. Then I backed up a few steps and stood still. He sniffed the water and lapped all of it down, while his eyes stayed trained on me. In those moments of watchful eye contact between the lion and me, I think he understood I was there to help.

When he finished, I didn't know if I could retrieve the bucket. With the stick, I fiddled around trying to lift the pail and move it toward me. The lion helped by giving it a whack with his paw, and it rolled my way. I managed to lift it back to me, while the lion stared, losing patience with my bumbling, or maybe losing his tolerance of me altogether.

I retreated halfway to the trees and tried my cell phone again. This time I got a signal and placed a call to the nearest wildlife preserve. After I explained the situation, the wildlife ranger on the phone said they'd try to come today. I didn't tell them I'd shot the lion, only that I'd discovered him, and he might not live another day, even if I could protect him.

Going back to the Jeep, I brought out a folding canvas chair and sat down. I had the Winchester beside me in case I had to use it on another predator. With binoculars, I glimpsed his pride off in the distance. They were within hearing range of their old leader but kept away for their own safety. The downed lion would attract predators. Eventually, a lone, roaming male would attempt to take over his pride.

The lion had to be uncomfortable in the heat with no shade. I considered taking him water again, but he'd need it more a few hours from now. The lion looked to the right, seeming to hear something. In time, I heard it, too—the sound of a vehicle. The old boy tried to stand, but could only raise his front end, and even that was painful. My spirits brightened, expecting the wildlife rangers. Instead, it was Ralph.

I rushed up the trail and waved him to stop.

"What's up, little bro," he said after turning off the engine of his four-door Land Rover.

"I found the lion I shot last night. He's alive, and wildlife rangers are on their way."

"So, you can finish him off now, put him out of his misery," he said, ready to jump out of the Jeep. "I'm here as your official guide."

"No. Stay put. I want to save him."

"You're nuts. He's old and crippled. They'll tell you to put him down." Ralph, being at a higher vantage point, had zeroed in on the lion, using his powerful rifle scope.

"Don't shoot him," I warned. "If you shoot him, we're through."

"You making this your last stand?" He sighted down the scope, and I imagined he was testing me.

I ran in front of his Jeep and stood where I was blocking a clean shot. "If you want the lion, shoot me first."

As the words rolled over my tongue, I realized how childish I sounded for a forty-year-old threatening my fifty-year-old brother. But this was more than a fight over a lion's life. It was about our lives, too. I was tired of living in Ralph's shadow, being his cub.

Ralph scowled, then tossed his head back and laughed. "How 'bout I leave my Rover here. I'll even put a red scarf on the antenna to alert the rangers. Then I'll circle nice and wide around your 'friend' over there and join you for a beer. I have a few that aren't warm yet."

I just stood there dumbfounded while he tied up the scarf and motioned for me to come around to the driver's side. He jumped out, handed me a cooler from the back, packed his rifle over his shoulder, and said, "Don't worry. This is just in case we get charged by a herd of elephants."

Another hardy laugh, as we started toward my Jeep, and I told him I'd broken down. The lion never took his eyes off us.

I brought out a second folding chair, and Ralph settled in with his cooler between us. Maybe I was showing off or just trying to prove I wasn't a wuss, but I said, "My friend needs water."

Retrieving the pail and filling it with most of the water I had left, I took the "cane" and toted my "water brigade" in front of Ralph. "Watch this."

Ralph's eyes widened. "You can't be serious."

"I have my pistol if I have to use it, so I don't need backup. I've already done this once today."

It was different now. The presence of another man-made the lion uneasy. Did he recognize both of us from yesterday? Maybe recalled our voices? I didn't know, but I was willing to risk it.

I went through the same patient routine, and the lion, though now more restless and probably in much more pain, tolerated my generosity. He lapped up the water eagerly and then slapped the pail back toward me. I laughed, and he released a gentle sound–not a growl, more like he'd talk to one of his cubs.

Taking the pail, I backed away once more and kept a cautious eye while I returned to Ralph.

"I don't believe it," he said, "even though I've just seen it with my own eyes. Looks like you have a symbiotic relationship with Simba over there." He couldn't resist laughing. "He's protecting you, too."

"What are you talking about?" I heard a deep growl and looked back at the lion. He was warning a small pack of hyenas. Whether it was his threatening rumble or the two of us with guns, the hyenas sized up the competition and left.

"I'm proud of you, bro. That mangey lion isn't worth losing our friendship." He stood and gave me a genuine hug, as opposed to his usual clap on the back. Ralph was enough older to be my father figure now that our dad was gone. In recent years I'd thought of him as Hemingway in Africa. He had the same tall, husky frame, graying hair, roughly trimmed beard, and mustache. Plus, he relished being the center of attention. I'd thought of calling him "Papa" but wasn't sure he'd appreciate it.

"You taught me something today, kid," he said, as he finished his beer and started another.

I was still on my first, and it was lukewarm. "What's that?"

"First of all, I was wrong about you. There're a lot of ways to be brave. You proved that. And I don't know jack about a lion's mind." He chuckled. "I called the rangers again while you were watering Simba, and they're on their way. Told them what you'd done and that got them interested."

"Thanks, Papa," I said, and he smiled back at me. "I take that as a compliment. Just don't say it in front of others."

The rangers came and tranquilized "Simba," then loaded him in their trailer. It took four of us to get the old lion inside. The taller ranger, a Shona, said, "I've seen worse. I think we can save him. Another day and he'd have been killed or died from infection. Now about your broken-down Jeep; let's see if we can save it, too."

He called over the younger ranger who worked his magic and got my vehicle running in short order. "Not good to be out here and not know how to fix one." He grinned, and I tipped him generously.

They got into their Land Rover and hauled away the trailer.

"We should go," Ralph said. "Gotta keep track of how your new friend's doing." He paused and rubbed his scruffy beard. "You know, maybe your hunting days are over. With your new-found talents, you might be a darned good photo safari guide."

As we followed the rangers, I vowed not to hunt again. I wanted to save wildlife. I pondered Ralph's idea that I take tourists on photo safaris, but other words crowded his–words of a Kenyan guide I'd met on a photo safari.

"Each year more and more people come to our country, and we try to make them all happy. But what I am thinking is, are the animals happy?"

The Bitter Pill

Greg Picard

It was odd that Rick Jefferson would call Ranger Chris Becker on his cell phone. He knew they had exchanged numbers, but he couldn't recall Rick ever using it. He wondered if there was a fire in the park that Rick's California Division of Forestry Fire Station protected, but that should have come up on his Park's radio channel.

"What's up, Rick?"

"You gonna be around the office today? I'd kinda like to talk with you for a bit."

"Sure, I should be back there a little before five. I'm on my way to Region for a meeting right now."

"How 'bout I meet you at your office at five then. I don't want to take a lot of your time."

Chris hung up and sat, thinking about the call. Rick sounded a little 'off' for some reason. He couldn't put his finger on it, but somehow he just heard a different overtone to his voice. They'd talked several times on fire issues, and he'd sometimes stop when Rick's crew was washing down their engine at the Paso Fire Station and have coffee with Rick and B.S. with them all as they worked. Once they even washed his truck for him without him or Rick even suggesting it. Fire guys were surprising that way—a different breed.

His meeting at Region was tedious, and his butt was sore from sitting in the hard, plastic chairs all day in their conference room. He opened the truck's hot cab and ran the A/C for a minute before sitting inside. Once inside, the residual warmth on the seat from the day's heat relaxed his muscles. He leaned back and enjoyed it as the A/C vent cooled his face, and he wondered again what the mysterious reason could be that Rick wanted to meet with him.

Ten after five and the office was empty but for Chris, as he heard the heavy clomping of forestry fire boots on the wooden stairs to his office.

"I'm glad there's no one here but you," Rick said as he stepped through the office doorway. "I wanted to keep this between you and me if we can."

"Sounds ominous."

"No, just personal is all," Rick said as he sat and looked at the floor. "Seems that my son is doing drugs, among other stupid things."

"What kind of drugs? Do you know?"

"Started with pot. I raised hell with him over that and thought he'd stopped fooling with the stuff. Now it's worse. I found this in his bedroom." He shoved a tin foil wrapped object, and Chris peeled it open.

"Looks like Opiates," Chris muttered.

"Yeah, downers."

"The stuff's pretty addictive, you know."

"Yeah, that's what scares me most," Rick whispered. "Look, I am hoping you can give me some ideas on what to do here. I know you've got a daughter, and she's not that much older than my son, so you've probably been through this kind of stuff to some extent."

Chris had several thoughts at once. First, he was a police officer and had some obligations in that regard. Rick was making the mistake so many made of thinking of him as just a 'fern feeler,' and it put him in an uncomfortable position. Second was his thought that Rick wouldn't like what he was going to say next.

"If he's not obeying your standards and doing illegal stuff, you need to turn him in to the sheriff's deputies. The system needs to take control of him at this point with mandatory drug test monitoring and, hopefully, a good program of drug diversion to attend."

"But they'll just put him in jail, won't they."

"Not necessarily, if he hasn't done anything else criminally...has he?"

"Not that I know of...well, he got in a fight with his girlfriend, and she called the cops on him."

"Just an argument without physical abuse?"

"Yeah, screaming match out front of her house at midnight. Folks weren't home. Cops just told them to quiet down and for him to go home."

"All I can tell you is that the longer you allow the drug use to go on without intervention, the worse it will become."

"Yeah, I figured you'd say that." Rick paused and studied his feet. "I was hoping maybe if you talked to him?"

Chris sighed. "Rick, if I talk and look around, it might likely wind up in an arrest. I won't ignore things. Have you tried to get him into a program like NarcAnon or Celebrate Recovery? There's meetings for that all around for all ages. You'd be surprised what kind of and how many people struggle with substance abuse."

"I haven't directly suggested that. I figure he'd just argue and flip out."

"You've heard the term Tough Love I'm sure?"

"Yeah."

"I'll tell you a secret. It's not really called that because you are being tough on the kid, it's called that because it's really most often tough to do as a parent. And even tougher if there are two parents trying to do it—because one will often undermine the other."

"My wife doesn't believe he's doing anything serious."

"You showed her these pills?"

"Yeah."

"Then she's in a serious case of denial. You've got a problem. I hate to tell you this, but this could cost you your relationship with her, no matter how you handle it, and if something bad happens to your son, she'll likely blame you."

"You're not helping."

"I'm just trying to prepare you for the battle, just like they do with soldiers that might die. There will be consequences, even if you win."

Rick didn't answer; he just sat clenching and unclenching his fists.

"Rick, it really all boils down to how much you want to save your son."

"He's my son, and I love him. I can't have him ruin his life."

"He's still under 18, so there's that to consider. When he crosses that line, the legal consequences get way more problematic and lasting. Whatever you do, you should do it now." Chris was uncomfortable in putting himself in the position of telling Rick what to do. He seriously risked being blamed for any failures or unpleasant outcomes, and there was no guarantee that any of this would have a good outcome in the long run. Drug abuse was a hard enemy to defeat.

"Have you ever told him you would drug test him yourself

and he will suffer the consequences if he fails a test?"

"No, I've thought about it, though."

"What could you deny him that would make it worthwhile in his mind to stay clean?"

"His video games."

"Yeah, I guess I should have expected that these days."

"He loves the ones on war, like *Call of Duty*. We've forbidden him to play the trashy violent street crime ones, but who knows what he does once he's hanging out with friends elsewhere."

"Yes, it's tough. You have to partner with other parents on controls and limit his exposure."

"Finding other parents who'll do that and who have kids he wants to hang out with is the biggest problem. Plus, we can't monitor him once he goes to school. He hangs out with whoever he wants."

"Control what you can. He comes straight home or else, and he only hangs with friends you approve...preferably supervised in some way. The ongoing drug tests should help the most. Does he have a car?"

"Yeah, an old beater he's fixing up."

"Take the keys if he fails in meeting a requirement or a drug test."

"That's a problem since he needs the car to get to school, and both my wife and I work, so we can't usually take him."

"Okay, just take his video games then. You know all this stuff. What's keeping you and your wife from doing it?"

"We both are tired from long hours at work, and this all takes physical and emotional energy to keep up with every day. You know what arguing with a teenager can be like. I've had more fun catching rattlers and rabid dogs."

"Well, either you do it, or the sheriff's gonna haul his butt away at some point, hopefully not on a gurney with medics trying to save his life."

Chris couldn't help but wonder what was holding this man back until it finally hit him. "You're not on board because your wife is not on the same page as you are. Am I right? She's just saying kids will be kids and need to experiment."

Rick stared at the floor. "Pretty much."

"And you think she'll criticize you if you come down too hard on your son, maybe even dump you."

"Yeah," Rick whispered. "She's pretty liberal. Child of the 60s flower power movement."

"She does pot still herself, doesn't she?" Chris asked.

"Some. She doesn't do it in front of me. She knows how I feel about it."

"Did you show her the opiate pill?"

"Not yet. I just found it this morning. I figured to show it to her tomorrow when she gets home."

It took Chris a second to digest why the delay until he remembered that Rick worked 24's. "Maybe she'll be in your corner when she sees it?"

"Maybe." Rick didn't sound at all convinced. Chris wondered how much of the man's marriage contributed to his son's issues.

"Okay, I need to get home, Rick. Allie's probably home from school and wondering where I am. I don't have much more to offer anyway...except maybe 'handcuffs' if you need me to do that."

Rick slid the beat-up wooden chair back and stood. "You've been a help. I guess I've known all along I need to do the things you've said regardless of what Cindy's reaction is gonna be."

"Trust me; I know how that feels. It's easy for me to sit here and pontificate. I don't want to minimize that I'd probably be in the same struggle if I were in your shoes. I'd probably be a total mess."

"Thanks."

"I'll walk down with you," Chris said as he grabbed his briefcase, shoved some papers in it, and slammed it shut.

* * *

Chris considered sharing the conversation he'd had with Rick with his daughter, but finally decided it should remain confidential. He doubted sharing it would produce any illuminating insights, and it just would compromise Rick's privacy. Living in the backcountry park fishbowl made considerations like that important sometimes.

The next morning as he headed into the office, his scanner barked out a sheriff's all-points bulletin for a stolen vehicle, and the suspect was Rick's son, Troy. He figured Troy's father would be just getting off work at the station and heading home. Sure enough, he saw Rick's pickup coming at him as he passed Halloween Point, and he pulled to a sudden stop in the road. He hit his lights and waved Rick down.

"Morning, Chris, what's up?

"Pull over on the shoulder; I need to talk to you for a minute."

They pulled into what little space was available on the road shoulders, and Chris got out and trotted over to Rick.

"I just got a sheriff's call. It's a stolen vehicle report, and the suspect is your son. Do you have any idea where he is?"

"What the hell! No, I don't know anything about this!"

"The vehicle is a white 1992 Toyota Corolla. Ring any bells."

"Yeah, that sounds like his girlfriend's car." He sighed. "I talked to my wife last night, and she was pissed he hadn't come home as of midnight," Rick said as he pulled out his cell phone and dialed.

"Did, Troy make it home okay?" He frowned as he listened. "But he's still there now, right? Okay. Keep him there. Is Trina's car there...okay, go look...okay. Don't be surprised if the cops show up. Apparently, he took it without her permission. You might want to get some answers out of him before they do show up. I'm on my way home now."

"You okay, Rick?"

"Yeah, but he's done it now."

"Well, maybe it will finally give you the handle you need to deal with him better?"

"Yeah, maybe. I keep thinking of what he was like when he was a little kid. Happy, smiling, playing catch. What the hell happened?" he said as he dropped the gearshift into drive.

"You can pretty well count on the fact that the drugs had a lot to do with it. If you need anything, let me know." Chris said as he pulled away.

Rick could hear the screaming from the driveway even before he got out of his truck. He found Cindy leaning against the wall outside Troy's room. listening to his son's crying and screaming tirade about his girlfriend and how "

"I didn't steal her car."

What followed was a variety of four-letter word descriptions of her.

"She got mad at me at the gas station in Julian and told me I had to walk home the ten miles in the woods in the dark at 1 a.m. I took the car while she was paying for the gas, and came home, and left the bitch there."

Rick saw a foot-wide hole smashed in the bathroom plaster wall. He looked at his son's demeanor and agitation and was pretty sure he was high on something like meth. He kept saying he was going to commit suicide, and Rick was sure he'd be arrested for the theft and tested for drugs. In the variety of possible scenarios, it seemed like a good outcome in many ways. Jail might do him some good and give him a dose of reality, but one corner of his brain wondered if his son would in some sick way enjoy the boost in 'street creds' it gave him as a 'tough guy.'

Cindy was overwhelmed and speechless. Rick was about to ask her to come with him so they could talk when there was a loud knock at the front door.

"That's probably the cops," he said as he passed by his wife and pulled open the front door. Two officers stood politely, and the tall one asked as he looked at the three of them, "is, Troy home?"

Rick pulled the door wide and motioned for the deputy to enter, the other one followed, and a third came around from the back of the house and stood in the open doorway.

"I didn't steal her car!" Troy said. He laid out the same story he had told his mom, and the officers told him to stand up as they cuffed him.

"You took it without her permission. It's been filed as a felony auto theft. We have to take him in." The last was directed at Rick and Cindy.

The third deputy escorted Troy to the sheriff's bronco and buckled him in the back. The two other deputies stayed with Rick and Cindy.

"I'm sorry we have to do this. Boyfriend/girlfriend stuff is always a mess, but our hands are tied at this point."

"Will he be drug tested?" Rick asked.

"As a matter of routine, we'll do that, especially if you think he's under the influence."

"I'm sure he is," Rick said as his wife shot him daggers with her eyes. He knew he was going to pay for his 'tough love' on this one.

"How could you tell them to test him and get him in more trouble!" she screamed at him as the deputies pulled down their long driveway to the dirt road that led back to Highway 79.

"He's got to be responsible for his behavior. We've let him get away with too much!"

Her eyes seemed to turn to black carbon and burned into him as she said adamantly, "We need to bail him out then. He can't stay in jail with all those criminal scum!"

"I don't know about that. Perhaps it would do him good to feel the consequences of what he's done and think about it for a while."

"Well, if you won't do it, I will," she fumed as she stomped out to her car, slamming the front door behind her.

Chris Becker's words were prophetic apparently, he thought to himself. He didn't try to stop her. It wouldn't work anyway. He needed to prepare to pay for his decision. She'd make it cost him. He considered calling Chris but decided against it. It would just be crying on his shoulder, and he didn't need to start that.

* * *

His wife discovered how the real world operated when the jail virtually laughed her out of the building. They told her he'd be arraigned on Monday morning. She could find out possible bail status then. It was a very long Saturday to be hanging around the house, considering her mood. Rick went into work Sunday morning on his regular shift but felt the black cloud over him all day. By the time he returned home Monday morning, his wife had already left for court in the hopes of finding out Troy's bail eligibility. He waited around home and was surprised to see them pull up in the driveway just before noon.

"I can't believe they required a $10,000 bond for him!" Cindy said as she slapped her keys on the countertop.

"Sounds pretty low for a car thief, if you ask me."

"He's not a car thief," she yelled.

"Did they tell you what his liability is in this case?"

"No. What liability?"

"Sentencing. He could do up to 18 months in jail or prison and be levied up to a $20,000 fine."

"That's ridiculous!"

"It's the law."

The mood was dark all over the house, and Troy stayed in his room. Cindy barely said two words to Rick all afternoon. He managed to find out on the computer courthouse website that his son's next court appearance was the day after tomorrow at nine. It was his day off, and he figured he'd go.

Rick took his wife out to dinner rather than have her cook. Troy was morose and locked himself in his room. Cindy was more confused than ever. The boy she thought she had been raising wasn't the boy she was experiencing. She was angry and felt guilty at the same time. Some of it was guilt over feeling like a failure as a parent; some was guilt over how she had treated Rick over this incident.

"I have to apologize," she said as she sat down across from him at the kitchen table when they got back home from the restaurant.

"For what," Rick asked.

"You know what. I've been treating you like a bad father when you've been right all along. I feel so dumb and betrayed by my own son, and it sucks."

"Yeah, I get it. I'm pissed at him, and I love him at the same time. I feel like I still need to protect him from the pain he's going to suffer, and yet that's the worst thing I could do to him. He needs to learn consequences. I thought we taught him that, but apparently, it doesn't apply to the real world outside our home."

He got up to look in on his son to say goodnight and realized looking at the open window by his bed that the boy was gone along with his backpack and his duffel bag.

"Now what do we do?" she cried and leaned her head on her palms, shaking it slowly.

"Well, first thing is we tell the sheriff he's taken off. He's on foot. I suspect he didn't take his car because he thought they'd I.D. it easily. On foot, he has the ability to keep a low profile. My guess is he's headed somewhere else for help."

"Who would he go? Not the girlfriend certainly."

"No. I'm thinking one of his buddies. One who's a little sketchy himself."

"You mean like Freddie."

"That's exactly who I was thinking. The little twerp has access to a car. He used his grandmother's to run away from home last year. Remember, even though he threw his cell phone out in a ditch to be untrackable, they eventually found him in Colorado living with some girl, covered with a bunch of tattoos, and out of money whining to his grandparents for help.

"I never liked that boy." She tapped the table impatiently, ending it with a resounding slap on the Formica top with the palm of her hand.

"I know where he lives. I'll call the sheriff." Rick sighed as he rose. In the background, sirens wailed as the Julian Fire contract ambulance sped by on the highway. It was followed shortly by the town's engine company. Rick flicked on the scanner he kept at home out of habit as he reached for the phone.

"Can I speak with someone who can get a message to deputies to start looking for my son? He's disappeared, and he's just been released from jail on bond for car theft. I suspect he won't show up in court if they don't find him and at least return him home."

In the background, the voice on his scanner was the Julian fire captain…"fully involved front porch fire…looks like an explosion all right. Can we get a second alarm support from the CDF Station?"

Rick passed on the information about his son to the desk sergeant on duty who promised to put out an alert to pick him up.

"Depending on what the deputies find, they may want to take him into custody. I assume you want him back at home if they decide not to arrest?"

Rick took a second to actually think that over. "Yeah, we'll lock him down somehow here. We should have done better, I know."

"Okay, have a good evening, sir."

The address of the scanner fire call was repeated twice to the CDF company, and it tickled Rick's brain.

"Cindy, I think that fire is at that kid's house!" he said as he pointed to the scanner. "Get your coat!"

When he went in his closet to get his own coat, that's when he discovered the gun cabinet door jimmied and ripped halfway off and his .357 revolver and his .45 semi-automatic missing.

"Cindy!"

* * *

The scene was full-on chaos. The front porch had been blown to pieces. The remainder of the house had somehow ignited, but the fire was contained quickly by the responding fire companies. They couldn't see their son anywhere. He quickly ran to the ambulance, where the rear doors were still open. A deputy stood near the rear step bumper.

"Hold on, sir! You can't go in there."

"I'm looking for my son; I think he might have been here!" Rick yelled.

"There's two boys in there. What's your son's name?"

"Troy Jefferson."

"One we know is Freddie Hartwell, I recognized him from a few unpleasant dealings we had a while back. The other one we haven't identified. He's burned pretty bad on the face and unconscious."

"Can't Freddie tell you who the other boy is? Can I just look and see?"

"Freddie's not going to be telling anybody anything anymore; the other boy's gonna be hard to recognize what with all the burns. Let me see if the medics can let you in."

He disappeared inside, and Rick heard whispered words as the deputy re-emerged.

"They're gonna take the other one to the hospital in a second, so you don't have much time to look. He needs to get there soon, they think."

Rick wasn't prepared for what he saw. Troy's right forearm was gone. All his hair was burned off, and the facial swelling was starting and was terrible. He had an airway inserted, and two full bore IVs were hung and running, but he was recognizable, and he was sure it was the shirt he had seen him in before dinner.

"What the hell happened here," Rick asked.

They say it was an explosion on the porch where the boys were is all I know. We've gotta go, sir, he needs to get to the ER," the medic said.

"Sure, that one's my son, we'll follow you in."

His wife was standing with the deputy when Rick stepped out of the ambulance.

"It's him, Cindy. He's hurt pretty badly."

"Noooo," she cried out.

"Did you find any weapons with them?" he asked the deputy.

"Yeah, a couple of handguns. Why?"

"They're probably mine. Troy took them. Jimmied my gun locker. I'll pick them up later; I'm gonna follow the ambulance into the ER. Do you know what caused all this?"

"From what we could tell, it looked like they were making a pipe bomb on the front porch. Somehow things didn't go right, and it blew up. We'll know more when the arson team looks at it."

"A pipe bomb," Cindy cried as she looked at Rick.

"Let's go, honey," he said as he tugged on her arm.

* * *

"The arm has been shattered into several pieces. I am not optimistic about him regaining the full use of it, even if the surgeon is successful in reattaching it," the ER Doc said. "Blast trauma is very damaging to the tissues and vascularity. He has a concussion, but surprisingly, it seems not to have bled much. The facial injuries were superficial. We'll know more about the possible tissue damage to the brain when he wakes. Also, you should know that there was a significant amount of fentanyl in his system. Which we were able to eventually block by administering Narcan. However, it may have been beneficial in slowing the amount of bleeding in the brain at the time of injury, since it reduces blood pressure."

"What's fentanyl?" Cindy asked.

It's a synthetic opioid, and basically, about the strongest downer you can get, and it's starting to become available on the street these days.

"How long will it be before he's awake?" Cindy asked.

"That's difficult to tell. At least a couple of hours. The surgery to put the arm back together is quite complicated, as you might assume. Fortunately, it was intact and kept on ice right away. If I were you, I'd get some coffee and maybe some food in the cafeteria, if you haven't eaten. It's likely to be a long night for all of us."

Rick pulled out his cell phone when they sat down in the cafeteria with coffee and breakfast rolls ten minutes later.

"Who are you calling?"

"I need to tell the Battalion Chief to get a replacement for me on my shift. I'm supposed to be at work in six hours." Once he had his Chief on board with the situation and had coverage arranged, he wanted to call Chris for some reason. In some way, he thought Chris might want to know what happened...and on a deeper level, he wondered if Chris could help him make sense of this nightmare. He dismissed it as silly to think talking to Chris could make this better.

Nobody could fix this. The kid is just getting worse. Fentanyl for God's sake! He thought sadly.

As he sat staring at his coffee cup, he wondered if the deputy on scene had known there was a BOLO issued for his son. There was no law enforcement watching his son here at the hospital, so that alert obviously fell through the cracks. Probably for the best, under the circumstances. He'd need to let the court know Troy wouldn't be able to make his upcoming court date. Would he even still 'be Troy' when he woke up after the brain bleed. He kept wondering if he had done something wrong or failed as a father in some way. He couldn't help feeling like he was to blame. After all, protecting his son was his job as a father, wasn't it?

* * *

Chris scanned the headlines as he munched his Cracklin' Oat Bran at the dining table. On page two, there was a picture of a house, and the headline read Two Julian Youths Blow Themselves Up and Start House Fire. Below the headline in smaller letters, it read One Dead. The article didn't release any names, and Chris wondered who they might be. It did say they were making a pipe bomb.

An hour later, he had just sat down at his desk when his cell phone vibrated.

"Hi Rick, what's up," he said cheerfully.

"My son just got out of surgery. He ran away and with one of his friends and managed to blow himself up last night."

"Oh, God! How is he?"

"Still not awake. They're worried about brain damage and the use of his right arm, which had to be reattached."

"Jeez, Rick, I'm so sorry. How can I help?"

"Help me kill the scum that sells drugs around here. And for that matter, whoever sold TNT to those kids."

"He's one of the kids in the paper this morning that got blown up?"

"Yeah, stupid kids." Chris wasn't sure, but he thought Rick was crying. The line was silent for several seconds. "Cindy's a basket case," he croaked out. "I don't know what to do next."

"Where are you?" Chris asked.

"Still at the hospital...the Sharp's ER in La Mesa. Hopefully, he's coming out of recovery pretty soon, and we'll be in room 12."

"Okay, I'll be there as soon as I can get there." He took his still unopened briefcase and clomped down the stairs.

"Jane, I need to head into town. Not sure when I'll be back." He tossed the last words over his shoulder as he let the entrance screen door to the office slam shut. He decided to head back home and take his personal car, but he didn't bother to change into street clothes.

* * *

"Your friend Freddie didn't make it," Rick said to his son.

"I was with Freddie. I remember that much. Where is he? I got to his house, and he was on the porch...I think making something. I don't remember anything after that."

"Freddie died in the explosion."

"Explosion?"

"The doctor said amnesia for the event would be likely, Troy. You and Freddie apparently were making a pipe bomb on his front porch, and it exploded. Freddie is dead. You are very lucky."

"Freddie's dead?" He looked vacantly at both of them. The room was silent as he processed the information. Finally, he looked down and said, "My arm feels funny. It tingles and hurts."

"It will for a while. The bomb tore it from your body, and they had to put you back together." Cindy said. "We're so glad you are alive."

Troy looked at his arm, covered in bandages, and tried to move it and grimaced with pain.

"So why were you running away?" Rick asked the boy as his wife gave him a dirty look. "I know you bashed in my gun locker and stole my handguns and ammo, and I'm pissed. That was stupid. Running would just get you more jail time, eventually. What the hell did you think you were doing!"

"I was scared. I'm sorry. I figured I could sell one of the guns for money to eat and hideout. I was gonna keep the other one for protection."

"How long did you think that would last before they caught you."

"I wasn't planning on getting caught. I can take care of myself."

"Yeah, right," Rick sneered and plopped heavily into the chair next to the bed as the door to the room opened.

"How's he doing?" Chris asked as he closed the distance to the bed.

"You've already called the cops to take me back to jail," Troy moaned at his dad.

"No, son, I'm not here to arrest you. I'd like to help you if I can."

"Since when can a police officer help me."

"I have a friend who funds a special rehab program that helps people learn not to use drugs. My guess is you need it more than you think you do. I'm hoping I can, with his help, get the judge to let you do that program rather than sit and rot in jail for car theft."

"I don't need a rehab program. Why would you do that anyway? Why?"

"I've seen too many kids go down the path you're on, son. You're lucky to be alive. I bet your buddy on the porch was high on something when he was making that pipe bomb, too, wasn't he?"

"I don't know. I don't remember much. I remember I had gotten to Freddie's house, but that's about it."

"Was Freddie your drug supplier?"

"He'd let me have some of his stuff; I don't know who he bought it from. I've never connected with anyone who sells." Troy appeared to be concentrating on something, and the room went quiet. "You know, he was there in the ambulance with me."

"Yeah, it was sad," Rick said

"No, I mean, he was there, Dad. He talked to me."

"He couldn't have talked to you, you were unconscious, and he was dead according to the medics."

"He was there, and we talked. He was afraid. There was someone else there, and he told Freddie he had to come with him. Freddie was afraid."

"Someone else?"

"Yeah, a guy...or a voice maybe. I'm not sure, but he said Freddie had to come with him."

"Freddie wasn't happy about it, and I didn't much like the guy who was saying he had to come with him either."

"What else do you remember?" Chris asked.

"Well, there was another guy sitting in the corner of the ambulance watching. I thought maybe he was one of the medics, but it seemed strange that he wasn't doing anything. He just sat there and stared at me. Once he gave a really disgusted look at the other guy that told Freddie he had to come with him. Then he looked at me and said, "Millie Swanson. You still have a job to do, listen to her." Then he just got up and left.

"Strange."

"Yeah, it bothers me. I wonder what he meant about me having a job to do?"

"Probably just a dream, your mind was playing tricks on you while you were unconscious."

"I don't think so, Dad, it was so real, and I don't know anyone named Millie Swanson."

* * *

The rehab for Troy was grueling. It started a month after the incident. He was still troubled with burning pains in his arm and hands. The therapist kept pushing him to do things with that arm.

"You need to work it, and it will take time. Next week you'll start group sessions with others who've been injured in a variety of ways. We'll expand the types of exercises and the difficulty slowly over the next few months."

Months of this physical agony wasn't what Troy wanted. The pills barely dulled the pain, and the doctor said he'd have to be entirely off them in another week.

He wondered a lot during those physical therapy sessions if Freddie hadn't been high messing with explosives, would his own arm be uninjured, and would his friend still be alive now? At the same time, he sometimes desperately longed for at least the magical high the marijuana gave him, especially as the doctor's Fentanyl started to wear off. That stuff was golden!

He was mulling these kinds of thoughts over while pulling a weighted cord in agony, even though it was no more resistance than pulling a set of Venetian blinds up. He desperately wanted a toke.

"Hi, how long have you been working on your arm today?" the young girl asked him as she walked into the room. She held a clipboard and pen and smiled at him. She wasn't someone he'd seen before and looked too young to be one of the doctors or nurses.

"I don't know, it feels like hours, but probably has been about ten minutes now."

She gave a little laugh. "Yeah, I imagine it can be pretty grueling. I brought you a treat. Take a break," she said as she handed him a Mountain Dew.

"It's my favorite, how'd you know?"

"Just a good guesser. You look like a Mountain Dew kinda guy." Her smile crinkled the corners of her eyes. She reminded him of an elf in Lord of the Rings, though he couldn't exactly say why.

"Thanks. Can I quit now?"

"Not hardly!" She laughed again. "You want to have that arm be the arm of a football quarterback, you'll need to double down, mister!"

"I'd settle just to be able to pick up my backpack and put it on myself."

"You going hiking?"

"No, it's how I carry my school stuff."

"Ah, yes. What grade?"

"Twelfth."

"College plans?"

He sighed. "Maybe community college. My grades aren't that good."

"Funny, you seem like a smart guy to me."

"How could you tell that in just, what, three minutes?"

"I'm very perceptive. For instance, I know your name is Troy Jefferson."

"Yeah, you just read that off of a chart somewhere."

"See, I told you that you were smart!"

"Doesn't take smart to figure that one out. You work here and have access to all the information. So what's your name, since I don't have a chart and you don't have a nametag."

"Well, smarty, I don't 'work' here, I'm a volunteer in my nursing work-study program. Millie Swanson," she said as she reached out to shake his hand.

Troy's throat was suddenly dry, and the pins and needles weren't just in his arm at this moment. He sat there with his mouth half open and felt perspiration bead on his forehead. His breathing quickened.

"I can shake the left hand if that's easier," she said when he didn't reach to shake hers.

Troy didn't move.

"Is something wrong?" she asked. "Are you in pain?"

"This can't be happening..." he croaked.

Troy had never thought much about supernatural things. Religious tales especially were a subject that wasn't much discussed in his home or among his friends except to mock it. Yet he couldn't explain the stranger in the ambulance and now this.

"Should I go get the physical therapist?" she asked.

"No, um, it's okay. I just was surprised?"

"About what?"

"You won't believe it. Hell, even I don't."

"What?"

Troy took a deep breath and steadied his hands. Even his lousy arm was shaking. "When I was unconscious in the ambulance the day of my injury, there were men in there that weren't part of the crew. One told the other kid who was hurt that he'd have to come with him, then as he was leaving, the other guy said I would meet "Millie Swanson...and I should listen to what she tells me."

"You sure you didn't imagine the whole thing."

"Anything's possible, I'd been doing drugs, and I was pretty high. But why would I imagine your exact name? I've never heard of you or met you. It makes no sense."

"Did your friend hear him say it, too?"

"Freddie was dead the whole time."

"What?"

"They said he was dead when the ambulance personnel got there, and they concentrated on me. But Freddie talked to me and this guy in the ambulance. He was very much alive. And the guy said I'd meet...you. And here you are. What the hell am I supposed to do with all that?"

"Were the ambulance guys there the whole time?"

"Yeah, but they acted like they didn't hear him."

"Do you believe in God? Angels? The Devil?"

"I don't know what I believe. Most of it sounds pretty far-fetched...curing blindness, walking on water, raising dead people, and coming back to life yourself. Dead people are dead."

"You said you were high. Do you have a drug problem?"

"Only when I don't have drugs," He gave a slight laugh that turned to a frown.

"You should talk to my pastor; he runs our drug rehab program, too. He might be able to explain what happened to you in the ambulance that day."

"I don't know if I want a sermon."

"Are you that scared?"

That got to his male ego, and he said, sharply, "I'm not scared! I just don't go for all that Jesus stuff."

"Look, you had something really strange happen to you that you can't explain. Why not talk to someone who deals with that kind of experience."

"I don't think so."

"I thought the guy said you were supposed to listen to me and do what I said."

Troy didn't have a good answer for that one.

"My pastor runs a 12-Step program for substance abusers that meets every Wednesday night at the church on C Street in Julian. It's filled with people who struggle with drugs, alcohol, and sex issues. I'll go with you if you want.

"Why would you go with me?"

"Well, somebody's got to protect you from all those Jesus freaks. They might make you cry..."

"Okay, I get it. I'll see what it's like, but if I don't like it, I'm outta there."

"Fair enough." She smiled. "Now, let's get back to the game of 'no pain, no gain!'"

* * *

Troy's parents were surprised when he said someone was going to pick him up to go to a church meeting after dinner. Actually, surprised didn't even come close to describing their reaction.

"A church?" his mother asked in disbelief. Cindy was a hardcore agnostic. Rick wasn't sure what to believe but thought most of it was a fairy tale, and it was more about control than anything else.

"Yeah, it's for people who abuse substances. Some kind of 12-Step program," Troy said.

The quick look and head shake that Rick gave Cindy was enough to quiet the ridicule he knew she was about to put forth. He figured 'any port in a storm,' and Troy needed something right now to give him direction away from drugs and the bad behavior that came with it. Rick knew he couldn't change his son, just maybe...God really could.

* * *

The setting was informal, and everyone was sitting at a table finishing pot luck dinner items they'd all brought to share. Troy grabbed a piece of chocolate cake and poured coffee into a paper cup before he sat in a corner seat next to Millie. "You all eat pretty well. Do they do this every week?"

"Yeah, pretty much. We'll start in a few minutes and have a little session together before we separate into men's and women's small groups. There's a new member's group the first night for you to attend briefly where they go over the basics. Then you can join the men."

He looked around the room. The men ranged from the early 20s to ones that looked like they were retired. It surprised him that someone that old would have substance abuse problems. As he reflected on that, he realized that at his core, he thought that no one survived through continual addiction to be that old. It shocked him a bit, and he wondered what kind of life these men and women had lived.

The general meeting began with introductions. Each one, as they went around the room, would give their name and their abuse issue.

Some were there because they had a family member who was addicted, which explained some of the 'old people,' but a couple of the old men were still struggling with serious drug and alcohol addictions. Two that sat in the circle said they were sex addicts as well as alcoholics. Four were women who were married to addicts on one was there because she told everyone she was a food addict. This wasn't quite what he had expected. Millie told the group that her father was a recovering heroin addict.

"What's recovering mean?" Troy asked Millie as they broke up to go to their men's and women's groups.

"Once an addict, always an addict."

"No! That's crazy."

"Crazy true, I'm afraid. You fight it for your whole life. Go do your orientation group, and I'll see you at eight when this ends," she said and gave him a gentle shove. He felt the familiarity of the shove, and the sensation was oddly nice.

Later, when the men's group was finishing up, the old guy leading it said something that made Troy sit up and listen.

"Addiction is all about relationships. If your relationships are bad or rocky, you go to drugs and alcohol for relief. If you are addicted to drugs or alcohol, your relationships go to hell. You then go to drugs and alcohol for relief. It's all about having good relationships." The regulars in the room all nodded like they'd heard it all before, almost like it was their motto or their 'charge' as they went forth. Troy thought about it, and the more he thought, the more sense it made. Freddie was in a bad relationship. His relationship with his parents wasn't that good either. Perhaps there was something to this meeting idea, after all, he thought as he walked to Millie's car.

"Well, how'd it go?" she asked as she cranked over the motor on her beat-up old Toyota.

"Okay, I guess."

"You guess?"

"The guys were nice enough, and I didn't feel weird. The Jesus stuff at the beginning of the program with everybody wasn't my thing, but I get the twelve steps idea."

"Every twelve-step program is the same as this one and is based on a higher power concept, even the non-Christian ones. The idea is, you can't do it alone."

"They did say something in the men's group that I liked...it's all about your relationships. Good relationships keep you out of trouble."

"Pretty good advice," she laughed. "Maybe you'll make some good relationships in this group. You know they aren't all radical Jesus freaks if that scares you."

"Stop sayin' I'm scared. I'm good with this," he said rather anemically.

Millie just smiled, dropped the car into first gear, and revved the engine as she pulled out of the lot.

* * *

Over the next few months, Troy began to enjoy and even look forward to the sense of community in the recovery group. They were all supportive and encouraging, and he could say anything he felt in the men's group...something he could not do at home with his parents. He also found himself drawn to Millie, even though she was a year older than he was. He didn't have the courage or even the first idea how to pursue that, though. They talked together at the coffee shop in Julian, often after the Monday meetings. She said she was in the group because of her father's addiction, but he suspected she got the fellowship and community benefit first and foremost. It had to be the real reason she went, and she was way too perfect to be an addict of any kind.

The most significant change in his life was the fact that he hadn't used any drugs since the night of the explosion and fire. He wasn't sure if it was the tragedy, the recovery group, or his infatuation with Millie. He had managed to graduate high school with a 'B' average and had applied to the Community College in El Cajon. It would start in September and was a long commute, but his parents were supportive. He was getting along with them better than he ever had, too.

He hadn't shared with his parents that he had begun to believe that the Christian faith might have some merits. He had been reading certain parts of the new testament that Millie had suggested, and it especially made sense on how to 'love your neighbor.' He was even ready to concede; there might be a God. He could never reconcile the men in the Ambulance that night any other way than something God-driven, and if that were true, he would be stupid not to learn more about it. He still wasn't sure about Jesus, but he learned there were several men back then who said they saw him alive, and they died rather than say he didn't come back from the dead. They certainly believed it, so he was ready to suspend judgment and at least learn more and also hang out with his struggling recovery group friends.

The oddest thing was Millie. He had never figured how to make a move on her and tell her how he felt...and; she saved him the trouble one recovery meeting night after coffee when she kissed 'him' goodnight.

He had read once how Jesus had been betrayed with a kiss, but somehow he didn't think it was like the one Millie gave him.

Highway Robbery

Dennis Royalty

The professor marched to the front of the room, papers stuffed under an arm.

Creative writing students perked from slouch to straighten. This was a big day in Rocky Blodgett's English 131 class.

"Rocky" was my nickname for Prof. Blodgett. I can't recall why, or his actual first name. But I do remember this particular day more than most in my college career.

Thirty-some of us were about to learn our grades for the first assignment of the semester. We'd submitted compositions the previous week, striving for clever, profound, fresh, or whatever else would register favorably on Rocky's big-stakes homework.

The stakes were big because he'd let us know that there would be just two lengthy papers to produce over the bulk of the semester. Each would be worth 25 percent of our letter grade. The remaining 50 percent would hinge on a paper assigned and written, start to finish, during the two-hour final exam.

I'd seated myself in the front row. As I watched Blodgett weave through desks, delivering graded papers, it was easy to read faces as students learned their marks.

I was confident my grade would be respectable. (Hey, I majored in journalism.) But my curiosity switched to concern when Rocky returned to the front of the room to begin lecturing. He'd handed back everyone's paper but mine.

I rose to ask why when he stopped me, turning to address the class.

"I'll start today by reading the most outstanding essay," he said, now sitting erect. He fingered the bridge of his glasses, took a deep breath, and began.

The first words seemed familiar. Then, it became clear. These were *my words.*

Classmates didn't recognize the mystery author, of course. Yet I felt embarrassed while Rocky read on, and especially at the end when he left his seat and ceremoniously dropped the paper on my desk with an encouraging, "Well done."

Rousing applause followed, echoing throughout the halls of the building.

Not really.

Still, this was an ego-enhancer, welcome in my early college days of highs and lows (see also: Economics E 201, and Psychology, P101).

Back to Blodgett's classroom. A month later, following the second 25 percent writing chore, it was *déjà vu.* Sort of.

Assignment 2 had been in his hands for a week. Once again Rocky strode briskly to the front of the room, 30 or so papers arm-crooked for the trip.

Pausing briefly to straighten the pile, Rocky once again weaved through our desks. Once again, looks of anticipation adorned faces. It was easy to tell who was pleased as letter grades dropped in front of classmates, or to read disappointment from others.

Once again, I'm seated in the front row. And, once more, Blodgett seems to have left papers with every person except me. Then he headed back to the front of the room to pronounce, once again, that a single paper stood out. We must all hear his reading of this exceptional writing.

Expectant eyes turned in my direction. Aw, shucks. Here we go again.

But...but....as Blodget read on, those *weren't my words.*

Huh? This time Blodgett crowned a female classmate the next acclaimed writing champion.

That's OK, I guess, but where was my paper? I had to wait through a 45-minute lecture to find out. When class dismissed, I confronted him.

"I returned all the papers I had," he said. "Are you sure you turned yours in?"

("Oh, yeah, Blodgett, I decided to skip this paper after I aced the first one. It's just too humbling when you keep reading my stuff out loud.")

Thankfully, Rocky couldn't hear that thought bubble.

"No, I turned it in," I managed. "I wrote this one even better than the first."

Rocky said he'd go through his office desk and check at home, too, in case he'd misplaced my work.

No luck. He'd lost my paper, though he never admitted it.

"I will accept your word that you turned it in," he said. "We'll judge you for the semester with your first paper and the final."

This plan concerned me, even though I was riding the A train. A misstep on the exam would send my grade the only direction it could–lower.

But the decision was locked in. My accomplishments would ride on just two grades.

There isn't a happy ending. Rocky Blodgett judged my final exam as B-worthy, making the course grade a B-plus. This was the outcome for one of only two students who had a creative writing paper judged so good that it was read to the entire class.

Unfortunately, at that time the university counted a B-plus as a grade of B on my transcript. B-level grades earned the equivalent of 3 points out of 4 on a 4-point scale.

Highway robbery!

Never mind the blanket A that I was awarded in another writing course by a very charitable professor or some "minus" grades that were rounded up in my favor over my college career.

You did me wrong, Rocky.

Where's the Fire

Cordell Compton

I was lying in bed one night thinking about a new story to write, and I described a childhood memory to my wife. The events occurred during my junior high school years, so I suppose that qualifies as "childhood."

My birth occurred during the early re-election campaign of President Harry Truman. I was born at my parent's house several months before Mr. Truman's stunning upset of Thomas Dewey, whom the whole country was just about to inaugurate as president since the election was as good as over as everyone well knew. Everyone, that is, except the voters who chose Mr. Truman.

The neighborhood in which I grew up was a working-class area in western Louisville, Kentucky. There were some retirees in the area, but most folks worked either in shops, retail stores, and factories. In the 1940s and 1950s, Louisville was still predominately an industrial city of modest size, almost 370,000. Significant employers included Ford Motor Company, which had two plants, International Harvester, American Standard, and various distilleries. The prominent tobacco companies such as Philip Morris, Brown & Williamson, and P. Lorillard had multiple factories in the area.

Mom was a stay-at-home mom, not uncommon in that era or so I thought. She was a former elementary school teacher who "had to retire" in the 1920s when she married my Dad; those were the "rules" of the school administration at that time. Mom was a Kentucky native, and Dad migrated to Kentucky from Mississippi. Dad's older brother was stationed at old Camp Taylor during World War I; he almost deployed overseas when the Armistice came through. He looked handsome in his doughboy uniform.

My uncle found employment at the B.F. Avery Tractor factory after his military discharge. Eking out a living in rural Mississippi in the 1920s was tough. Steady work in the "big city" was attractive, so Dad ventured north. A larger farm implement company, Minneapolis-Moline, bought the factor in 1951. Dad was an assembly line worker who sometimes got "piece work" pay instead of "day work" or regular hourly pay. Despite his best efforts to explain that nomenclature, I did not understand "peace work." *Did they have fights in the factory, and you got more pay for not fighting?*

Sadly, the plant closed in 1955, throwing Dad out of work. He was 53 at the time with a grade school education and few marketable skills. The characteristics and qualities of mechanical skills, integrity, and intelligence (gumption, he called it) did not easily translate during a job interview. Eventually, he found work at various jobs and retired in 1971 from a valve and fittings plant that also made package boilers where he worked for fifteen years.

My older brother and only sibling married when I was age nine. That event transformed me into the "only child" status. He needled and pestered me continually as provided in the Older Brothers Handbook. I did not miss those times. Usually, a tussle would break out, which raised the ire of our father. There was always an invisible, unknown flash point beyond which his nerves could not tolerate our shenanigans. His temper blazed intense and hot when we breached that hidden point.

One memorable moment of tussling took a terrible turn. My brother had me in a headlock from which I loudly protested and attempted to escape. Somehow, we knocked over a lamp and broke the glass shade. Pop was reading the evening paper and instantly slammed it to the floor. He always propped his legs on one of the kitchen chairs while reading as a poor man's recliner. This time, however, he jumped up, grabbed the chair with both hands, and slammed it onto the bed that separated my brother and me on one side from Pop on the other side. Whether we would see our next birthday was in considerable doubt at the moment, but we survived.

Those events I did not miss. Since I was the only child in the household, I buried my head in books and magazines to pass the time. I remember enjoying the monthly *Reader's Digest.* I do not remember the advertisement's sponsor, but the gist of the ad was to encourage reading. The critical line in the full-page ad was: "People who read more, achieve more." I'm not sure how much I have achieved in my lifetime, but I absorbed a variety of material.

On the northwest corner of Main Street and 34th Street, the old Louisville Fire Department had a staffed, two-story firehouse. Our house was two doors away and also had a second story, albeit shorter than the firehouse. After my brother married and moved away, I inherited the upstairs front room, which served as a combination bedroom, TV room, and sitting area. My single bed faced the window where I usually lounged during the day reading and watching the traffic below. When the fire engine left for a call, I could look out as they roared past our house.

During my brother's post-high school years, he would hang out occasionally at the firehouse and became acquainted with some of the day crew. One fellow, an engineer, was a favorite. He repaired watches while he sat at the duty desk and worked on our father's watch.

Louisville firehouses had a ticker-tape mechanism that displayed fire alarm box numbers when an alarm box was "pulled." Each station had a card index showing the location of the alarm box. When an alarm came in on the Joker System, as the Louisville Department called it, the device would then punch out the box number on the ticker tape. A horn or claxon sounded with each punch. The punches were shaped like triangles with a space between each "number" punched. A series of punches such as: ◀◀◀ ◀◀◀◀ ◀◀ indicated box number 342 on a particular street corner; the card index gave the cross streets. The new ticker tape unwound from the right side reel, through the punch mechanism, to the left side take-up reel. Fire personnel stored and archived the tapes to maintain a record of the alarms.

The alarm notification system used in Louisville was most likely the Gamewell System named after John Gamewell of South Carolina, who purchased regional rights in 1855 to market the system and later gained full rights and patents in 1859. Those rights and patents, unfortunately, were taken away during the Civil War. John Kennard, however, bought the patents from the government and returned them to Gamewell in 1867 when he formed a partnership with Gamewell. The Gamewell Fire Alarm Telegraph Co. emerged in 1879.

During the summer, when the windows were open, the ticker tape alarm claxon was easily heard at our house less than two hundred feet from the firehouse. More often than not, I would walk to the firehouse, get the alarm's location, and ride my bicycle to the area if it was not too far away. If I waited too long to check the tape, the large overhead firehouse door would close, so I'd have to enter through a side door. The firemen were considered our neighbors, and no one in the area even thought of damaging any firehouse equipment or disturbing their personal belongings when they were on a fire run.

The engine assigned to our firehouse was called a Quad engine. That is, it had pumper capabilities, a booster tank filled with water, a hose bed carrying hundreds of feet of fire hose, and multiple ground ladders. The truck had a two-seat open cab for the driver (usually the engineer) and the duty captain. During a working (active) fire, the engineer stayed by the pumping controls on the driver's side of the truck to monitor and adjust the water pressure to the hoses. During a working fire, the firemen (no women yet) connected a large house to the nearest fire hydrant, and the other end connected to the Quad engine. The engine's pump boosted the water pressure to smaller hoses manned by the firemen spraying the fire.

The other firefighters, usually four or five men, sat on two bench seats atop the engine behind the open cab. The bench seats faced either side of the truck. They rode almost side-saddle one could say. During my grade school years, the firehouse crews had a small, black dog as a mascot who jumped on the engine and rode to each alarm. The little guy was a Standard Manchester who yapped as the truck left the firehouse. I always thought his yaps meant, "Faster you guys, faster, we've got a fire to put out!"

Eventually, my "childhood" fire engine was replaced in the mid-1960s by a newer unit. It was still a Quad engine, but the crew firefighters had to stand and hang on the back of the engine. The driver and captain again rode in the open cab. Since the driver and captain could not see behind them when they were in the cab waiting to leave, the crew firefighters pushed a buzzer on the rear of the engine, indicating everyone was on board. The truck then roared out of the firehouse to the next alarm. Sadly by this time, the mascot, Cricket, had transitioned to Mascot Heaven.

Research indicated my childhood fire engine was a 1930s Ahrens-Fox unit manufactured in Cincinnati, Ohio, just up the river from Louisville. With my attraction to the firefighters and their equipment, I am amazed that I did not pursue a career in firefighting. Had that occurred, I would have remained in the Louisville area and followed a different career path in life.

The Joke's on Her
Sharon Sterling

Two men meet in a bar. One is a young military reject with delusions of soldierly machismo. The other is a white-haired snob who harbors family-induced delusions that he is well-bred.

Business is slow tonight at the roadside establishment called the Outlaw Lounge, a sleazy watering hole enveloped in a beer-scented bubble. It squats on desert hard-pan beside the main thoroughfare. Each time a patron enters, scents of alcohol and despair leech out; creosote and desiccation creep in.

The week-night bartender reveals his inadequacy to the demands of life with slumped shoulders, an undernourished body, and decayed teeth. Humming a song, he comes wiping the bar down toward the white-haired snob. He looks at the man's nearly empty glass and asks, "Another Scotch for the road, Mister Hotchkiss?" He hums the tune louder.

The gray-haired man recognizes the tune then remembers the lyrics, something about a girlfriend and more booze. His woozy brain decides to take it personally.

He takes his elbow off the bar and sits up straight. "You cretin. I never drive drunk."

The barkeep shoots him a thin-lipped grin. "I reckon you don't, Mr. Hotchkiss." He sings a bit of the lyrics.

Porter Hotchkiss snarls at the barkeep. "You idiot. Mrs. Hotchkiss is no one's baby."

A shrug rounds the barkeep's shoulders more. "If you say so, Mr. Hotchkiss. Never seen her here."

"Wilma wouldn't be caught dead in this place, you consummate bore. Even a good stiff one wouldn't make her happy tonight." Hotchkiss instantly recognizes his faux pas.

The barkeep's eyes flash with sly glee and he briefly reveals what's left of his teeth, the smile prompted by his obscene train of thought.

Hotchkiss attempts to derail the barkeep's train with a flood of words. "Wilma's latest book is driving us crazy. The publisher's deadline is next month and she's worked up over the jacket. She needs a headshot for that. She needs a great headshot, and soon, damn it!"

The bartender's glance slides sideways toward the young military reject two stools down. Their eyes meet. The young man's eyes narrow as he looks at Hotchkiss. He eases over the empty barstool to sit next to the older man. He wipes glass-sweat from his right hand onto his pants and holds out the hand. He says, "Hi. Wolf Waringwerger."

Hotchkiss hesitates. He thinks, Wolf? Like Wolf Blitzer? Even so, this fellow is forward, a bit full of himself. He stares, not hiding his inspection of the young man. Wolf's dark hair is cropped close to the skull; his face is expressionless but beneath a black t-shirt, his biceps, triceps, and pectorals are well-defined. He wears camouflage-print fatigue pants and GI-issue boots.

For reasons that will bedevil him until the moment of his death, Hotchkiss yields to the workings of fate. He shakes the young man's hand. "Porter Hotchkiss," he says, doling out his name slowly, thinking the other man is surely unworthy of hearing it.

Wolf doesn't waste time. He says, "I overheard. You got a job needs doing? Your wife?"

"I don't imagine that's any concern of yours."

"It is if you're serious. Happens I'm an expert."

Hotchkiss sniffs. A whiff of smoke is irritating his nostrils, telling him this young man is addict to nicotine. He says, "I am always dead-serious, young man. Besides, you don't look mature enough for the artistic kind of thing we want. What have you done before? I certainly don't recognize your name."

Wolf swivels his barstool so his back is to the bar. He lowers his voice, which forces Hotchkiss to turn also. Wolf says, "I'm just now back on the block."

"What?"

"First civilian division.

"What?"

"You know, sofa squad."

"Pardon?"

Wolf barely conceals his impatience. He utters the required explanations in a patronizing tone with inflections of superiority that lend credence to his lies. "I'm a Marine. Combat decorated, just discharged. Between jobs now. My civilian work is better than good; I'm an artist at my specialty. "

"How good would that be?"

"My headshots are legend. I have a wide field of view. I'm good at positional shooting. I can do the work in any location, at any time, under any conditions including poor lighting."

Hotchkiss contemplates Wolf's verbal resume. He hears, emanating from deep in the recesses of his alcohol-infused brain, a warning--the annoying, tongue-clicking sound his mother and wife make when reproving him. He dismisses the peculiar omen as an artifact of too many scotch and sodas. He reassures himself that even though he's had a few, he will never be a sloppy, stupid drunk. He asks, "You can shoot in any location? Even at home? Actually, that might work. She doesn't want to leave the house, she's so busy with the conclusion of that blasted book."

Wolf anticipates a rapid closure to the pact. "Home is the best place. They're relaxed, the line of drift is limited and natural."

"Candid shots, hum?"

"You could call it that."

"But do you have the right equipment? Quality equipment is essential for professional results. We insist on the best, not some point and shoot hand-held."

"I have the best hardware around, two top-notch babies. The first is a Precision Templar V2 6.5 Creedmoor. My favorite, though, is my 700 BDL custom Poyer. Objective and ocular lenses, bipod, infrared, the works."

"Infrared?" Hotchkiss doesn't recognize the technical descriptions but he won't question this young Wolf, because that would reveal his own ignorance. He is impressed by the detailed, dead-on descriptions of photography equipment but more so, by the young man's eagerness to work.

Hotchkiss tilts his head and says, "We seldom deal with unknowns, but maybe you are the one to shoot frames for Wilma. Let's hope it turns out well. You know, when my wife talks about something splendid, she says, 'It's to die for'."

Wolf laughs, long and loud, startling Hotchkiss, who thinks, That was totally inappropriate. The man lacks class. He lowers the corners of his mouth and gulps the last of his Scotch before he says, "We haven't discussed details yet. How much do you charge?"

"Low ball, five hundred Benjamins. Top rate, one large."

Hotchkiss again is at a loss. "Would you mind not using that military slang? In plain English, please."

The put-down raises Wolf's hackles but in recent months, he's learned to suppress the dominant feature of his personality--rage. He says, "That's between five hundred to one thousand dollars."

"Rather steep! Tell you what, let's agree on five hundred, but I could go to seven if the work is done quickly and results are good enough."

Wolf's mouth hardens. "Cold barrel zero? I can do that. Five doubles will seal it, then just give me the address." The stiff-necked face staring into his wears a blank expression. Wolf says to him, lips tight, barely moving, "That's one hundred dollars--in twenties--if you have it."

"Of course I have it," Hotchkiss replies. He pulls out his wallet. He rubs each bill between thumb and finger before handing them to the young man. He thinks this is a strange place to do business. Still, I told my wife I would take care of her. As much as I sometimes hate the high-strung harridan, she probably deserves it. Hotchkiss hands Wolf his business card then opens his own hand. Wolf hesitates, gets it, says, "Oh, sorry. I'm out." He pats his pockets as if assuring himself he has no business cards. He pulls out an old bar tab, scrawls his name, the address of a downtown bar, and the number of his latest burner cell phone.

Hotchkiss climbs down from the barstool and surreptitiously steadies himself before he says, "Fine, young man. We must proceed as quickly as possible. I'll call you."

As soon as Hotchkiss is out the door, Wolf turns to the barkeep. "What a dickwad."

"Yeah, a real bag of smashed a-holes. Hey, Wolf, I never saw that tattoo on your arm before. What does FTA stand for?"

"Stands for f--- the Army and the Marine Corps and the whole f---ing military. F--- Hotchkiss and his cranial rectosis, too." Wolf slaps money on the bar and stands abruptly. "Got to un-ass. Gonna grab a pump-and-dump with the bitch. Then at zero-dark-thirty, take care of business. A deal's a deal, even with a douche-bag, bone-head like Hotchkiss."

* * *

Jimmy Smith, aka Wolf Waringwerger, has the good sense to leave his battered pickup truck on the outskirts of the upscale neighborhood. He carries his equipment, broken down into manageable pieces, in a harmless-looking pack slung over his shoulder. He is dressed in black. When he is well into the neighborhood, he pauses and smears his face with a piece of charcoal. Now he is virtually invisible as he strides to the address of the Hotchkiss home. He is sure his approach hasn't been spotted.

The sprawling, ranch-style structure of glass and stone is insulated from its neighbors by rows of shrubbery and stands of huge cacti. Wolf-Jimmy stows his bag beneath a well-cared-for hedge, then circles the house, looking into curtain-less windows. He quickly identifies his target and sets up the shot.

Unable to take the preferred prone position due to the closeness of the target, he takes the alternate stance, attaches the infrared scope, and loads the frangible bullets. Cold barrel zero, one-shot only for the seven hundred dollars. He aims. Only a window and a wisp of sheer curtain separate him and the target.

Aim. Steady, hold his breath, squeeze. Crack! The Glaser bullet fragments on impact. Wolf-Jimmy sees the woman's head explode in a burst of bone, blood, and brain tissue. The pink cloud! He celebrates silently, thinking "Woohoo!" He read about the pink cloud in combat magazines. Grinning, he crouches and slinks away, breaking down the rifle and stowing it in the backpack while on the move. A block farther on, he strips off the black shirt and hat, tosses them into the landscaping, wipes his face clean, and becomes just a man out for an evening stroll. The sound of sirens makes him grin. A string of drool slips from the corner of his mouth.

* * *

Morning newspapers scream headlines about his one-shot victory, calling it vicious and deadly. There is a suspect on the loose. Jimmy shakes his head. Not a word of appreciation for the suspect's (his) expert marksmanship. Why hasn't Hotchkiss called by now about delivering the six hundred owed him? He chain-smokes as he paces an alley not far from the Outlaw Lounge where this cluster-f... began. Uncertainties tear at him. Did Hotchkiss go to the address he printed on the bar tab to pay him in person? He'd check it out. On the way on foot through alleys and back streets, his phone rings. He keys it on, "Yeah?"

A voice says, "Hello. Is this Wolf?" It's not the voice of Mr. Hotchkiss. Alarmed, he says nothing. He dumps the burner phone into a garbage can and stalks on. More than a block away from the other bar, the one on the bar tab now in Hotchkiss-Dickwad's possession, he spots a police patrol car parked in front.

Fury. Fury floods his pale face with color. Dickwad turned on him, ratted him out to the cops so he wouldn't have to pay! He turns back toward the Hotchkiss house. He wants to go back, beat the six Benjamins out of the &%$#*&%! Through clenched teeth, he mutters every curse word military troops have ever coined.

Kill Hotchkiss! Ah. But risky. Too risky with cops in it. Logic soon overtakes rage. He thinks, Lost this one for sure. Can't win them all. Skip town. Yeah, someplace where cops and news vultures don't freak out over the death of one old civilian split-tail. Yeah. Write it off. He remembers the pink cloud with a chuckle. Remembering it will be his payoff.

Arranged Marriage

S. Resler Nelson

Listening to her parents debate in the living room, Anna trembled. They knew she was pregnant. She stood in the dining room of the old farmhouse and caught glimpses of them as they argued. Anna was losing favor with her father, despite her mother's pleas.

"Henry, please talk to her."

"There's nothing to talk about, Ruth. Anna has sinned, and now she must pay."

Anna looked out the dining room window and stared at her father's beloved fields of corn. It was 1920 in the Midwest, and her father was a third-generation farmer, a staunch Christian, and a devoted husband. But flexible, he was not. He had stern standards his children must follow, and Anna had violated both her father's and mother's unspoken rule about sex out of wedlock. She'd heard the scriptures, too. What she'd done was fornication, unclean, and against God's will ... at least in her parents' eyes, though her mother was begging for leniency.

Furthermore, it was the father's right to approve his daughter's marriage. That meant the future groom should request Anna's hand in matrimony, by formally asking her father for permission to marry her.

Anna's mother started to cry, and Henry said, "All right, send her in."

Ruth called out, and Anna slipped into the room, head down, dreading what was coming. Her mother retreated to the kitchen, her bidding over. Now it was just Anna and her father. Henry noted his oldest daughter's dishwater blonde hair, her homemade dress, and her shy eyes, red from crying.

Anna's brothers and sisters were at their aunt's house for the afternoon. She assumed her parents had arranged it, so they could have time alone with her.

"Your mother has told me of your sin," Henry said. "Now what are you going to do about it?"

"Father, you don't understand. Adam loves me and wants to do the right thing. He wants to marry me, and I know we'll be happy together. We'll make you and Mother proud," Anna said, though, in her heart of hearts, she doubted her father would bend.

"When is this child to be born?" her father scowled.

"In about seven months," she whispered.

"You're only sixteen. Not even out of school, and neither is he."

"I will have to drop out, but he can finish and then work at the feed store for his dad," Anna explained since she and Adam had discussed all this.

"Why isn't he here?" her father barked.

"He wanted to be with me and to ask for your permission, but when we told Mother, she said I should talk to you first ... alone," Anna said sheepishly.

Her father looked to the kitchen and yelled, "Ruth! Get in here!"

When Ruth returned, Henry admonished her. "So, you were planning behind my back?"

"No," she said, unsteady. "I just thought we should talk to Anna before we spoke to Adam."

"And what are your brother and sisters to think, Anna? How's this going to sit with our friends, our relatives, and our Pastor?"

Henry was clearly agitated, with clenched fists and a reddening face.

Anna wanted to shrink into a corner or run away. Her father wasn't abusive–not any more than other fathers who spanked or punished their children. But he was unrelenting. Once his mind was made up, there were no compromises. Surely, her mother knew that.

Her father stood, and his tall, strong body towered over Anna. "I forbid you to marry Adam. Why should he be rewarded for what he's done?"

"But Father, we love each other," Anna beseeched him. "Will you deny us and the baby that?"

"Yes," he said firmly, even as his wife looked on in disbelief and disgust.

"Henry," Ruth disputed, "are you going to force Anna to have the child out of wedlock? Forbid them to marry? Where will Anna go?"

"They should have thought of that before they sinned," Henry huffed. "I may have some answers, but it will not include Adam. One who cannot even provide for a wife and child."

Ruth made one last argument. "Henry, when you and I married, we had to live on *this* farm with your parents while you worked the land with your dad. You didn't have money, either."

"That was different," he scowled. "We obeyed the Good Book."

"And they will, too," Ruth ventured.

Henry turned his back on both of them, charged out the front door, and headed for the barn. It was time to feed the livestock.

Two days passed, and Henry summoned his wife and Anna into the living room once more, while the three other children played at their aunt's house again. Henry had refused to talk to Adam or Adam's parents. Henry had declared to Ruth, this was his problem to resolve.

Now his wife and daughter stood before him with solemn faces and drooping shoulders, but Henry seemed relieved. "I have a solution," he announced. "It will be good for all of us."

Ruth appeared reassured, but Anna looked nervous and skeptical.

"I have talked to our friend, Gabe, and he will marry Anna–right away."

Anna covered her mouth to avoid screaming. Gabe was widowed, but he was her father's age. He seemed nice enough, but she could never love him–not like Adam.

"Henry, isn't Gabe too old?" Ruth protested.

"He has wisdom on his side, and Anna could use some of that. He will be good to her, treat her well, and he has the land and means to care for her and future children.

Anna cringed. Surely, her father couldn't be serious. And if he was, this was some sort of twisted punishment. She seethed inside but said nothing. He wouldn't listen anyway, his conviction firmly in place. She ran crying from the room.

Within the month, Gabe married Anna in a small ceremony at the church, attended only by family members. Anna stayed home on Gabe's farm through most of her pregnancy, through birthing and beyond, so that when she appeared in public, the rumors would be that she must have gotten pregnant on their wedding night.

Gabe and Anna proudly showed off their delicate daughter, Maryanne. But Anna never erased Adam from her mind, and she avoided going to the feed store where she might encounter him. They didn't attend the same church, and a year later, she heard that Adam was planning to marry one of Anna's former classmates.

Anna and Gabe had five other children, but to Anna, her Maryanne was special–the one conceived through innocence and love. However, as Maryanne reached her teens, she became a rebellious child, as free-spirited as her mother had been when she met Adam.

One dark, wintery night, when Maryanne was a junior in high school, she got into an angry fight with her mother. Maryanne announced to her mother that she was going out with an older boy, who had a car. "Johnny is taking me to the movies tonight."

"No," Anna said. "I haven't even met this 'Johnny.' You've told me very little about him, except that he's four years older than you."

Saying no to Maryanne escalated immediately into a contentious fight.

"Keep your voice down, Mary," Anna scolded. "Your father isn't feeling well and has gone to bed. You are staying home tonight. Ask Johnny to come in, so I can get to know him. That's the least you can do."

"Our plans are made, and we're taking a friend of his, too. I *am* going, Mother, and you can't stop me. You can meet Johnny before we drive away, but we're running late."

Maryanne stormed out of the house to wait for Johnny on the porch. Anna left her alone to brood and maybe see her point of view. Meanwhile, Anna busied herself in the kitchen, fearing if she talked to Maryanne on the porch their argument might resume.

The boyfriend drove up in a pickup, and Anna stepped outside to meet him. A guy, likely Johnny, was behind the wheel, and another young man accompanied him. The truck door opened, and Maryanne climbed in and over him, to sit between them.

A strong foreboding gripped Anna, but before she could even say anything, Maryanne waved, the truck door closed, and they sped away, streaming into darkness.

An hour later, police arrived at Anna's door with the news there'd been an accident. Maryanne had been killed in a car crash, the only one of the three occupants to die. She'd plunged through the windshield.

Anna crumpled to the floor in a flood of tears and moans. She'd not only lost Adam; she'd now lost their beautiful daughter—the daughter she cherished. And Maryanne's last memory of her mother was a dreadful fight.

This is a true family story. I have changed the names, of course, and had to fictionalize the dialogue since the full story is sketchy. The arranged marriage was real, as was the tragic ending.

Seventh Grade

Mike Doyle

I couldn't wait to be a 7th grader at Sacred Heart School in the Bronx. Once that day arrived, I never wanted it to end.

Looking back, it was the sweet-spot as a pre-teen and it is one of the most cherished times of my life.

We finally had The Brothers as teachers. I truly admired these men, these educators, these role models. I had even seriously considered becoming a Christian Brother, envisioning myself as a teacher in SHS when I would finally come of age. These men understood the boys and had no problem letting us know that they were in charge. I could relate to them so much better than I could relate to the priests and the nuns. They commanded our respect and we wanted to do right by them. The brothers got involved. The other clergy members generally had no interest in you unless it directly involved the Church or Catholicism.

It is not my intent to disparage any of the other dedicated teachers that I had before this. As a matter of fact, I had so many excellent teachers all the way through grammar school. Namely, Brother Benedict, Mrs. Fuery, Ms. Welby, and Mrs. McNamara, who is my all-time favorite.

The only horrible experience I had at Sacred Heart School was in the second grade. However, that's a whole other story.

As it was, the LaSalle Christian Brothers, a religious order of Catholic Monks who taught in the segregated boys' section of the school, were no-nonsense, strict, firm, and (mostly) fair. I loved how they got actively involved with the students in sports and activities outside of the classroom. You would see them in Ogden Park playing handball and blackball. Or you'd see them in the school gymnasium coaching the basketball teams after school and on Saturdays. And when weather permitted, you'd find them coaching track and field events near Yankees Stadium at Macomb's Park.

It was a splendid time to be in Sacred Heart School. That place, that era, the fall of 1964 through the spring of 1965 was very special to me.

I could be mistaken, but I seem to remember the fall lasted longer that year and the air was sweeter. I think we had a double Indian summer. And winter was short-lived. Even the springtime seemed to begin earlier. Admittedly, this is my paintbrush with broad colorful memory strokes.

The winds of change and the sands of time hadn't affected us back then. We still had our innocence. Our neighborhood, HighBridge, was still relatively intact. Most of our neighbors still lived in the apartments they had always lived in. We were wrapped in a warm blanket of familiarity, comfort, and stability.

I loved my newly assigned seat in our homeroom class along with the windows that faced east. My prior seat was front and center of Brother Jerome. He had a splashy habit of giving you the weather when he spoke with passion. He spoke with spittle. I would have preferred having a windshield or a silly umbrella hat to protect me when he gave a dissertation on a story from the Old Testament. When he spoke of Jonah, you experienced the ocean. That was our fall semester Religion class.

The spring semester religion class was the New Testament, but I didn't have to weather those storms. By that time, I had my new seat by the window. Just dreaming my days away.

I sat midway down the last aisle near a row of windows. We had those heavy desks that were screwed to wooden runners in sets of three.

Ah! I remember the heat from the steam radiators in front of the windows. Roasty-toasty warm in the winter. I would gaze out the window, half-listening to Brothers Jerome, Thomas, and Raymond.

My eyes would find their way past the Church near the school, the Convent with its Belgium Block archway and gated entrance between the school and the Church. Across the street stood the Highbridge Public Library, another wrought iron gated fortress. If I turned my head to the left I could see the 168th Street City Steps and my early childhood apartment house at 1234 Shakespeare Ave. Beyond those immediate sites was the Jerome Ave Elevated Subway shouldering the # 4 train. When the classroom windows were open, you could hear the distant rattle of the train.

Looking eastward, past the elevated iron train structure, were the Grand Concourse, Long Island, and across the Atlantic Ocean, Europe.

Obviously, the imagined views of those farthest points from my window seat existed inside my head. Although I could not see those faraway lands and their peoples who spoke in foreign tongues.

I knew those tall windows were mine to behold, to stare off into the distance, and to wonder.

When I was offered the opportunity to move up to the 'A' class, I politely declined. I told my teacher, Brother Jerome, that he should offer that transfer to another student, maybe Dicky O'Connor, a kid who had been my classmate since the first grade.

Besides, I didn't want the pressure and competition of the 'A' class. At the end of the semester, we all took the same final exams printed on the aromatic mimeograph paper. Although, I do recall that the Diocesan Final Exams were printed on some very boring official-looking black-inked parchment. The paper just didn't smell as good.

In truth, I just didn't want to give up my seat, my cozy spot, my burrow. There was no need to learn my lessons any faster than I was capable of absorbing them. Thankfully, Brother Jerome took my suggestion. Dicky never knew that I had passed that opportunity on to him. Besides, one student had to leave our B Class because another one was being jettisoned in from the A-Class. It worked out fine for me, as I became very good friends with that other student, who shall remain nameless.

I felt that the 'A' class would have moved along just a little too fast for me. I knew that if I got lost along the way, I would remain lost and be too embarrassed to ask a question for fear of sounding dumb. Back then, and still, until this day, I need to learn at a slightly slower pace. Nothing proves this more accurately than my trying to keep up with the speed of today's technology.

Besides, I liked being among my classmates: Jimmy Moore, Richie Cullen, Billy Berkfeld, Dicky Nielsen, Frankie Zieran, Ray Duffy, Michael Pearson, and so many others. It was comfortable and it felt safe. There was never any bullying, never any fights. Everyone got along.

My class job was to walk up and down the aisles at the end of the day with that army-green colored wastebasket so the kids could toss their daily collection of debris. Someone else had the job of 'clapping the erasers' on the back steps. Someone else had to clean the blackboard. I'd get hit in the face or the chest with balled-up sheets of loose-leaf paper and an occasional tissue full of snot. The trash carrier was a human basketball backboard. Never malicious, all in good fun. Oddly enough, years later, I worked as a part-time janitor in both schools. It would bring back boyhood memories as I mopped and swept the same aisles that I walked up and down for eight years.

I had several crushes that year that carried well over into 8th grade. There was Terry Fagen, Loretta Rivers, and Mickey McNulty to name just a few. Their last names have been changed to protect them from embarrassment. Although, I hope that if they read this, it brings a smile to their faces. Of course, they never even knew I existed, but those boyhood crushes were wonderful. Had they ever spoken to me, I would have been a tongue-tied babbling idiot. I was quite shy. But, the infatuation was real.

One of the things I relished most about this grade was that nothing was really expected of us. There was no pressure other than to pass your classes. The real pressure was on the 8th graders. Co-Op exams, hoping to get into the Catholic High School of your choice. They were getting ready to leave the nest.

I was comfortable being sandwiched between the lower grades and the 8th graders. Nobody took notice of us. We were kind of invisible. I also knew that 8th grade would mean having to say good-bye to the kids you spent eight years with. I hated good-byes back then and I still do today.

I often wondered why a neighborhood as densely populated and isolated as HighBridge didn't have its own High School. Our High

School could have easily been built years earlier on Brown's Hill, where the New York City Housing Projects had been built. I remember seeing George Washington High School on the other side of the Harlem River in Manhattan and wondered why we couldn't have that?

A second opportunity was missed when they didn't build a High School on the site of the Old Little League field on West 166th street between Ogden and University Avenues. Such a perfect location! Right smack dab in the middle of the neighborhood. It was within walking distance of all the blocks in the neighborhood and the #37 City Bus stopped on the corner of 166th Street and Ogden Avenue. Instead, they erected a 25 story monstrosity of an apartment building. All I ask is; why was that necessary? Who decided that we needed to travel more than an hour each way to the High Schools we would end up attending?

I was quite content to remain in our Concrete Camelot, our Shangri La. This was our own Little Village nestled high in hills and dales of our Bronx Highbridge neighborhood. I didn't need or want the outside world.

But such is life. I revere my Sacred Heart/HighBridge upbringing. I love the past, but I also look forward to what the future has yet to bring.

The Last All-Nighter

Dennis Royalty

They call it cramming, pulling an all-nighter, "waiting till the last minute" or more simply, procrastination.

Ranking the silly things I did in college, all-night studying for a final exam neared the top.

Doesn't work. Didn't work. Not for me.

Tom Benton and I knew we were in trouble as our final neared for the "History of Western Civilization." So we staked out a dorm lounge, bought snacks, and settled in for desperation mode.

"Benjie" was a flop-haired guy who looked like a high school junior. Fifty years later, he's probably still yanking out his driver's license to earn senior discounts.

Studying came easily to him. So why were we a pair that night?

In 1968 I was a sophomore, he a freshman. Like me, Benjie had overestimated how prepared he was in Western Civ. Studying for other finals shoved this one to the back burner.

Hoping you can cram everything you need to know into six or seven hours is foolish. But we were headstrong dudes. Never mind the text was huge, telephone-bookish. We were convinced that by7:30 a.m., we'd be ready.

And so we crammed. A lot of serious work happened in the first hour or two, from maybe 10 to midnight. We quizzed each other, reviewed earlier tests and assignments, and strained to remember what the prof had emphasized. Determination reigned.

Staying up late wasn't all that unusual for college types, so we figured this would be a walk in the park. The clock passed 1, then 2 before fatigue began to take hold.

A bathroom trip found the hallways quiet. Doors were closed and slumber ruled for sensible people. Envy brought temptation: let's give it another hour or two, catch a nap, and head to the final.

But we kept on. That's because our studying made it painfully apparent that what we didn't know reached swimming pool depths.

So, can't stop now. Can't stop until it's time to head to Ballantine Hall.

Concentration waned. First, the atmosphere turned giddy, humorous. Then it shifted to testy, argumentative. Lack of sleep drained any spirit of goodwill.

With class notes spilled across tables, chairs, and ottomans. I'd strayed across the room, leaving my book behind. I asked Benjie to hand it over.

"Get your own," he snapped. On second thought, he grabbed the text and flung it my way, with force.

Pages tore through the air. Dozens separated from the softback cover, unable to survive the cartwheeling journey in my direction. **I was furious.**

Expletive, expletive! I leaped up and grabbed what was left of the book, bounding toward Benjie. He'd pay for his insolence.

Then, in mid-charge, a revelation.

I noticed a name scrawled on the torn cover.

"Tom Benton," it said.

He'd thrown his own book at me.

My gleeful howl seemed to make the evening worth it. Not so.

We eventually dragged ourselves to the final, a 2-hour ordeal. All those facts about western civilization competed with keeping my eyes open. As I yawned repeatedly, a teaching assistant approached. Did I need some coffee?

The upshot: My performance cost me an entire letter grade for the semester.

I learned a lesson that had nothing to do with academics. It was a lesson in preparation, or lack of sensibly preparing. My habits had to change, and they did.

A wise colleague later described the importance of planning and personal discipline like this: "Allow yourself to fail–and recover." Great advice.

So, this was my last all-nighter.

Benjie? I bet he aced it. He was one of those fall-in-the-hay-find-pony types.

I would end this tale right here, but doing so without passing along another cramming episode would rob you of a story that makes me smile.

College buddy John Messina, still a close friend, relates:

It was my astrophysics final, A401 or A402. This was my major, so I wanted to make sure I was ready and really knew the material.

I had my own room, so staying up all night wasn't a problem. The final was at 7:30 a.m. the next morning. I kept studying until about 5:30 when I was satisfied that I was ready.

I decided to take a nap so I could be fresh. I'd get up at 7 and have plenty of time to walk to the test.

"But I woke up around 8:30! I was in a state of shock. Oh no! I may have missed the final exam in my major!

I don't remember if I'd forgotten to set the alarm, or if I just slept through it. But I dashed over to the classroom, now around 9 a.m. for a test that was supposed to end at 9:30.

I barged in and told the prof 'I'm so sorry. I overslept. Is there anything I can do?'

"I was feeling really lousy, especially when the prof, Dr. Honeycutt, said he'd take me to another room to work on it. I figured he'd make me do the entire test in 30 minutes.

But he didn't.

Honeycutt opened the door, and six other students were sitting there. Turns out we're all there for the same reason.

John and the rest got to take the test in full. Unlike me, he knew his stuff, from general relativity to problems involving gravitational orbiting to identifying different types of telescopes. His "A" locked in the same grade for the semester.

At least one of us had a happy ending.

The Bus

Mike Doyle

I held on tightly as we crossed Ogden Avenue at 168th Street on that day back in 1955.

Grandma was in an unusual hurry that Bronx morning.

I knew she and I were taking a bus to go somewhere, because she always had the bus fare ready in her right hand, holding the coins in a semi-fisted grasp. I think it was a dime back then because I seem to remember my mom complaining years later when the bus fare rose to 15 cents.

Grandma's pointer and middle fingers were firmly extended and my job was to wrap my three-year-old hand snugly around those two projected fingers whenever we crossed a street.

This day we were crossing a busy two-way street and there was to be no lolly-gagging. Just cross quickly.

It is only just now, as I write this sentence, that I've come to understand a flash-back memory that must have run through her mind every time she crossed the street near the Crown Drug Store.

Approximately three decades earlier, on November 22, 1927, her father was run over and killed on Ogden Avenue by a taxi cab just north of this busy intersection. I can only imagine that her father's tragic death must have crossed her mind every time she crossed that street.

In the 1950s and 1960s, I think Ogden Avenue and West 168th Street was probably the busiest intersection in our neighborhood. The # 11 and #37 buses joined routes at that point. At this busy cross-street, there also lived *The Green Dot Candy Store* on the southeast corner, which was a favorite hangout for the young teens of the neighborhood. *The Ogden Park & Playground* graced the northwest corner of the intersection, a place where you could find kids of all ages. And you'd also come across mothers sitting on benches with strollers or baby carriages gabbing with other moms. On the northeast corner stood the Crown Drug Store, at the time, one of the busiest drug stores in the Bronx. And on the southwest corner of the intersection sat Reilly's Bar, a very popular nexus for all ages.

I didn't know exactly where grandma was going that morning and I didn't really care. All that mattered was; I was with her and we were going on a bus ride!

But I do remember, there was a level of urgency in her stride. I did know we were headed over the bridge to 'The Heights' because of where we waited for this bus. If we were headed "Cross-Town" to 170th Street, we would have waited for the bus across from Sacred Heart School. I also knew of this other bus that often waited sleepily nearby on Nelson Avenue, facing away from the school. We didn't ride that bus back then and I didn't know where it went. Lots of the school kids took it, but it wasn't a yellow bus, which I knew were school buses. I only knew about the big city buses we rode.

I could sense her purposeful movements that day.

Anyway, along came the number 37 bus a minute later. I'm just guessing it was only a minute–as this three-year-old didn't know how to tell time. You could always see the bus coming from a few blocks away. The bus arrived and the doors opened wide. Grandma moved me in front of her and switched me to her left hand to help me up the steep steps.

The bus driver looked at me and said: "Well, look who we have here. It's Mickey Mike the Bum" and laughed.

I must have laughed also, and as I did every time I saw my grandpa, I know I said, "Hi, Grampa!"

My Grandfather was driving the #37 bus route that day. He loved to taunt me with that nickname and I hated it. And that's what Grandma's purposeful rushing was all about. She didn't want me to miss this event. Grandpa was driving our bus!

She dropped her coins in the chute and I ran to the back of the bus. She still paid her fare, even though her husband drove the bus. There was a perfect 'life lesson' planted in my brain by her actions at that moment.

The rear of the bus was my favorite place to ride. I vaguely recall an elderly woman saying 'Hello Michael" as I hurried by. Grandma knew everybody. That back seat was always so warm and cozy in the winter. Although it wasn't wintertime; on this particular day as I remember Grandma wearing a dress and no coat and her pocketbook over her shoulder. Not a fancy dress, just a grandma kind of a dress.

I loved to stand up and look out the back windows to see where we had been. I always got carsick in dad's car. But, never while riding in the back seat of the bus. Maybe I reasoned that looking back was better?

The bus climbed the hills and made a right turn where Ogden Avenue ended, near the bank, at the tip of our neighborhood, and then it went down the EL Grant Highway.

I could never understand why the bus had to turn away from the bridge, go down the El Grant Highway, and make a u-turn to go back up the hill to get to the bridge.

But, the exciting part was yet to come. We were soon going to cross the bridge over the river to that wonderland with the big stores called *The Heights.*

I would always ask if I could change to a side window seat as we crossed the bridge. I loved seeing our neighborhood bridge, *The Highbridge,* to the south.

I had a picture-story book entitled: *Who Built The Bridge?* and I would ask my mom to read it to me over and over and over again. It mirrored the story of our two bridges. A beloved, tired old bridge who had served her people well and a newer bridge that could carry the load of buses, trucks, and cars across the Harlem River.

Grandma let me change to a window seat.

I saw our tired old bridge, the *Highbridge,* and her majestic Watertower fade from sight.

My heart swells with joy and I love reliving this cherished little boy's memory of a time when I am three years old once again—and I still have grandma and grandpa in my life every day.

When Diego Fuentes Woke Up

Sharon Boerbon Hanson

A Children's Story . . .

When Diego Fuentes woke up, scarlet-feathered One-eye had not yet crowed the day awake. Diego stretched under his red woolen blanket. He rubbed his nose warm with the palm of his hand. A perfect morning to make hot chocolate to surprise Mama and Papa.

He rose and tugged his blue and red serape over his shoulders. He slipped his feet into his harrachis. Then he heard a voice murmuring low. It was Mama. "...about Diego," he heard her say. "He is so quiet, Papa, always writing. He never plays baseball. He never plays. He is so...so...different."

Diego did not hear what papa replied. He kept hearing Mama say "different." Diego sat on his bed and pulled his red wool blanket up to his face. Its familiar roughness comforted him.

"Different. Mama said I'm different
and different sounded bad.
But I'm simply me.
The only me I ever had."

Different churned in his stomach during school. Different prickled him like bits of straw when he swept out the chicken coop. Different trudged with him that night when he entered dream world.

When Diego woke up one thin cloth covered him. He heard Mama's voice, a voice familiar, yet not. Diego opened his eyes. The room, just one room, hovered close and dark around him. Tin and cardboard walls replaced adobe. He looked about and sniffed baking bread.

Mama, a mama familiar, yet not, crouched before dung embers that glowed in one corner of the dirt floor. Chapatis baked on the fire before her. "Up daughter, get up Shanti, today you work at the factory."

Diego-Shanti shivered. Her two sisters had already had left the charpoy, the rope bed they shared. She missed their warmth. They had already left for the factory. Today altered her life forever. No longer would she haul water from the city well with other young girls. No longer would she pound grain into flour with mother.

Today, she would earn money. Money to buy a school shirt. A shirt to allow her younger brother, Bilal, to go to school. Shanti pulled on her skirt. She nibbled the flat oval of bread mother handed to her. It tasted good, but she ate only half. She saved half for her mid-day meal.

The sun blazed, hot and round and yellow-white. Its rays reached down all the way into the narrow, crooked streets. Shanti wiped her brow with her skirt hem. She and her sisters would earn money to send Bilal to school. To help them all enjoy a different life, a better life, someday. Today her life was already different. Not better, not yet, maybe soon.

"Different. Life will be different.
A different I hope will be fine.
And now I'm doubled in strength
I've Diego's in addition to mine."

Different massaged her arms when Shanti hoisted heavy cloth bundles. Different growled in her stomach as day lengthened into night. Different cuddled her close when she slid into dream world. When Shanti woke up she was in a tangle of smooth, cool sheets.

"Wake up chattery sparrow, your soup is warm." Shanti opened her eyes. The sheet shimmered pale pink around her. She looked about the room. When she had fallen asleep, her charpoy, with sisters in it had sat on a hard dirt floor. Now a woven tatami mat covered wide wooden planks and she was alone. Then the wall moved.

Or rather, the thin sliding shoji screen that replaced the tin and cardboard walls, moved. The walls and bed were familiar, yet different, the aromas coming from a separate room were familiar, yet different. Shanti waited.

A thin, pleasant face peeked in. Mama. A mama familiar, yet not. "Kimiko," she said, "up, daughter, get up. It is six o'clock already. Hurry, hurry."

Diego-Shanti-Kimiko stared at Mama as she turned and left. Cram school - special Saturday school started today. Kimiko jumped up. She pulled on the green kimono laying at the foot of her floor mattress and left her small bedroom. She padded quietly to the main room. Kimiko bowed good-morning to Papa. Kneeling on the floor cushion before the low table she began to eat her miso soup and rice.

"Our little bird does not chirp as usual today Papa," Mama said. "Perhaps she takes studies seriously today. Perhaps she practices listening," Papa said. "Perhaps she will act differently and make us proud after all."

Kimiko peered at Papa from her big brown-black eyes and finished eating breakfast. Papa had said different would make him proud.

"Different. Papa hopes I'll be different.
So different doesn't sound quite so bad.
And now I'm more than only me.
I don't feel so sad."

Different buzzed through her head on the train to cram school.
Different chased her fingers as they flew through piano lessons.
Different sailed with her when she slipped into dream world.

When Kimiko woke up, the scent of stewed green bananas curled through the house. "Muhutel, Muhutel, wake up sleepy boy. Today you leave the village." Diego-Shanti-Kimiko-Muhutel opened his eyes. Sunlight filtered here and there through the woven branches and mud that formed the walls of the low-roofed hut. Today, the men of Kamba tribe held rites marking boyhood initiation into manhood.

Father sat on the floor with his three wives. They all gravely watched as Muhutel rose and wrapped his leather skirt around his dark waist.

"Today son," Father said, "you woke in your seventh summer as a boy. Tomorrow you will wake in your first summer as a man. Life holds learning and responsibility. Life shall be different for you."

Muhutel savored the breakfast stew, steaming in the carved bowl that Mama handed him. Tomorrow he joined other new men tending small herds of goats, learning to plant cassava, and finding out the secrets of wood-carving. A new style of life. A different, exciting style full of the interests of men.

"Different. A life interesting and different.
Different helps me feel great.
Yes, now I am many and mighty,
Different sounds like a good fate."

The thought of different lightened his feet as he left his village for the ceremonies. The thought of different comforted him through the long day of secret rituals. The thought of different cushioned his head when he entered dream world.

When Muhutel woke up, night still hugged the sky. The aroma of breakfast tortillas browning on the fire filtered into the bedroom. Diego-Shanti-Kimiko-Muhutel tossed off the woolen cover and bounced out of bed. "Mama! Papa! he shouted as he ran from his room. Up to Mama he darted and kissed her cheek. Words tumbled from his tongue and spilled into the new day.

"This morning I will take Maria Luanna to see if the cactus by the cornfield has buds. I'm going to Grandmama's hacienda and take eggs to her. Tonight, I write a poem just for you."
Mama smiled her big wide smile. "Diego," she exclaimed. "What has gotten into you this morning? My talented, different little love."

Diego smiled. If mama only knew what had gotten into him. He hugged Mama tight. Today he knew that different didn't mean bad. Today he knew that different didn't mean good. Today Diego-Shanti-Kimiko-Muhutel knew different simply meant—not the same.

Biographies

Roger Antony grew up in Maryland and began writing stories at an early age. He graduated from the University of Maryland with a Bachelor's degree in Civil Engineering and an MBA. Early in his career, he had the opportunity to spend four years in Columbus, Mississippi working on the locks and dams along the Tennessee-Tombigbee Waterway. Columbus is the setting for three of his twelve novels. His genres include science fiction, historical fiction, mystery, suspense/thriller, young adult, and romance.

Dee Cohen is a poet, fiction writer, and photographer, currently living in Prescott AZ. Her work has been published in various journals, books, and newspapers. Her story 'By Heart' was selected for inclusion in The Best Small Fictions 2015. Her poetry chapbook, Lime Avenue Evening, was published by the Laguna Poets.

Cordell Compton retired in 2012 from a forty-year career that focused on customer service and financial management both in KY and AZ. Cordell then began researching and writing historical fiction short stories based on past encouragement from high school teachers and college professors. Two of those stories have been published in the 2018 and 2019 Central Arizona Writers anthology editions. His ultimate goal is to collect and publish all of his short stories and novelettes. He is enjoying married life again in Concord, NC.

James Downey—After earning a BS degree in Psychology and a thirty-year career as an attorney, Army veteran James Downey changed direction, veering into the world of authorship. The events of 9-11 and lingering questions about human behavior prompted his first two books. The Evolution of Jihad, written under the pen name of H. Davidson, explores how the search for the one true God of Abraham evolved into the terrorism we face today. His second book, Why?, tackles the question of why the world is so full of suffering if there is a God who loves us.

A two-year project to capture some of the rapidly-vanishing stories of the valor and courage of our veterans and war survivors led to his third book, Brothers in Arms, which captures memoirs from WWII, the Korean War, and Vietnam. Containing 130 photographs and document reproductions, Brothers in Arms was awarded a five-star rating by Readers Favorite.

Mr. Downey enjoys motorcycling, scuba diving and travel with his wife, and spending time with their eight grandchildren. Trips to far-flung destinations such as Fiji and Eastern Europe, including the underbelly of Russia, and recently to Israel, Jordan, and Egypt, created a growing appreciation for the life we enjoy in our country.

Mr. Downey's books are available on Amazon. The link to Why? And Brothers in Arms is amazon.com/gp/product/B0846459NY.

Pat Fogarty is an editor, award-winning author, and poet. Pat is a graduate of the Creative Writing Program at Yavapai College. Born and raised in the South Bronx, his works are infused with personal experiences from his childhood. He writes Creative Non-fiction, literary fiction, and poetry. Pat's stories and poems have been published in a plethora of magazines and journals—locally, nationally, and internationally. Threshold—the literary magazine of Yavapai College, Inscape—the annual literary magazine of Washburn University, and Tincture—Australia's Literary Journal are just a few of the publishers who have featured Pat's work. His short stories have also been included in several anthologies. Pat is the Editor & Publisher of the AZ Writers Best Short Stories, Best Poems, Best New Short Stories, & Best New Poetry series. Pat retired from the International Brotherhood of Electrical Workers in 2005 after 35 years of service. He is also an accredited Alcohol and Substance Abuse Counselor as well as a Certified Union Counselor. He is currently the President of The Central Arizona Writers and past president of the Professional Writers of Prescott. Pat is happily married to his soul-mate Susan, and together they enjoy spending time at their home in the Mountains of Central Arizona with their German Shepherd and three Irish Terriers.

*"Bronx Girls Gone" by Pat Fogarty is available at Fine book stores across the USA, the UK, and Europe. Also available at: https://www.amazon.com/Bronx-Girls-Gone-Murder-Murders/dp/1950105075/ref=tmm_pap_swatch_0?_encoding=UTF8&qid=1606249136&sr=8-2

"Bronx Boys Gone" by Pat Fogarty Available at Fine bookstores across the UK, Europe, & the USA. Expected release date March 15, 2021

Sharon Boerbon Hanson,

the published author of 13 non-fiction books, as well as poetry, dystopian flash fiction, and editorial commentary, wrote a career success blog for eight years. Her travel memoir *See, Do, Be, Learn, Live,* and fantasy novel, *The Straits of Allback,* are currently undergoing preparation for publication.

An award-winning public speaker, her web site and social media efforts are underway. The holder of an MFA in writing, she offers developmental editorial services. You may contact her at writerinmn@gmail.com, with "Dev Services Request" in the subject line.

Susan Lanning is the published author of mystery and suspense novels. She was an English teacher in Ohio and since retiring to Arizona has taught novel and fiction writing to would-be authors. She's a member of CAW, AAUW, and Suspicious Characters. And in her spare time works lights for her husband's productions at PCA. You can check out her books on Amazon.

Dan Dražen Mazur is a Croatian-born American writer who has lived in Prescott since 1992. He has published a total of 10 books: four poetry books, two books of short stories, and four novels. He currently works on his third novel about his anti-hero character named Spinner Walker: *Spinner and the Duke of Prunes; Spinner and the Wrath of the Mandrill,* while the newest one has the working title *Spinner and All or Nothing.*

S RESLER NELSON has been writing throughout her life, creating short stories and poetry since she was Sandy Resler, a teenager in Redding, California. A graduate of San Francisco State University, she taught high school English, journalism, and art in Oregon. Her other pursuits were showing horses and oil painting. Also, she and her husband, Paul, led photo safaris and group tours on six continents. They live in Prescott, Arizona, with two beloved Shetland Sheepdogs.

Her first novel in the popular Luke Hudson Mystery Series is *More Than Dead,* published in 2015, followed by *More Than Gone, More Than Bad, More Than Lost,* and *More Than Dark* in 2020. Each book is a stand-alone and fans appreciate Nelson's crisp writing style. They are available on Amazon, Kindle, Good Reads, and in bookstores e.i. The Purple Cat. Email Sandy at sreslernelson@outlook.com to have her visit your book club, do a book signing, or other author presentations.

Greg Picard finished his Bachelor's Degree in English, specializing in creative writing. After getting his Masters in education and counseling, he worked as a high school and college teacher, counselor, park ranger, editor, firefighter/medic, musician, railroad brakeman, and historian as well. He has written travel articles, humor books, mysteries, and a book of short essays and cartoons. He makes his home in the Rocky Mountains.

Dennis Royalty is a retired reporter/editor/columnist who moved from Indiana to Prescott Valley, Arizona, in 2016. He is a business-journalism graduate of Indiana University.

Dennis spent nearly three years as a sportswriter for the former Bloomington (Ind.) *Courier-Tribune* after graduation. He then worked in several capacities for *The Indianapolis Star* for 27 years, including as a reporter, city editor, bureau chief, and columnist. In 2001 he joined Eli Lilly and Company (also in Indianapolis), retiring in 2015 as managing editor for internal communications. Dennis and his wife, Ginger, have a son and daughter who live in the Midwest. Contact info: Dennisroyalty@gmail.com

www.ingramcontent.com/pod-product-compliance
Lightning Source LLC
Chambersburg PA
CBHW021326190726
48288CB00003B/973

* 9 7 8 1 9 5 0 1 0 5 1 6 8 *